Objections Handled!

101 Sample Scripts For Network Marketers
Learn To Say The Right Thing To Every Prospect

By Monte Taylor, Jr.

www.montetaylor.com

THANK YOU!
Thank you for downloading my book.
Please be kind and REVIEW this book on Amazon. I welcome and need your feedback to make the next version even better.

To receive free "off the grid," prospecting tips, reports, and more scripts," plus a FREE video series designed to help you get full value from this book, click or go to the link below to subscribe:

www.montetaylor.com/freestuff

Dedicated to Tom and Bethany Alkazin.
They are two of the most positive and generous people I've
had the pleasure of knowing.

By example they have taught me to focus on helping others, to
become a student of the industry, and to never give up.

Acknowledgements

I'm especially grateful to those who have had a positive impact on my life and in ways they may or may not realize: My beautiful wife Penny who has supported me unfailingly in all my business endeavors – some successful and others not so much.

My steadfast business partner John Souza - a difference maker in this industry; My son Eric, a wonderful communicator, energetic spirit, leader and rising star; Brad Alkazin who has led the way and shown everyone who's paying attention that young people, with big dreams, can build outrageous businesses; the amazing Todd Smith who points the way, gives generously of his time and leads by action and example; Mike Sheffield, Garvin DeShazer, Ken Lind and all the SRN team who have helped thousands of entrepreneurs achieve their dreams; uncommonly great teachers: Bob Proctor and Dr. Joe Vitale; an extraordinary executive and industry thought-leader – B.K. Boreyko.

Lee and Fabio Okubo who epitomize servant leadership, determination and a willingness to help others; my friends including the amazing Clint Holmes; Jane and Ken McCoy, Bill and Debbie Phillips, Karen Boita, David Hernandez, Dick and Becky Groves, Dr. Robert Keller and Dr. Peter Lord for their continual support; Larry Weeks and Bruce Stafford for sharing their stories, laughs, tears and friendship; Mother Joanne Bourg for instilling her competitive spirit. Judy Torres for always "being there" for the family.

Allen Willey, the consummate communicator and co-host on hundreds of conference calls; Rachel Kelders who personifies determination, spirit and gratitude; Steve Sitkowski for his unflappable style, salesmanship and knack for keeping things real; my lifelong friends, Fred and Tracy Montilla, Bruce and Vicki Benge who exemplify a positive attitude, style, and humor; my sister Suzzanne Stanford, the model for, "Do what you say you're going to do;" Marilyn Lahr, a shining light for empowering female business women; my children Nick, Andrea, Chris, Eric, Austin and Delaney who amaze me with their talents and ability and keep me laughing.

TABLE OF CONTENTS

INTRODUCTION

My sister surprised me one day.

Darlene is a true extrovert. She loves people. She enjoys conversation with friends (and strangers) and is not afraid to express her opinion about almost anything. To describe her as outgoing would be an understatement.

She has watched my network marketing adventures over the years and knows it's possible to make a full-time income in the industry with part-time effort. She understands it can be challenging yet rewarding. She's also heard me speak often about how fulfilling the business is and how easy it is to develop rich and satisfying personal relationships with so many positive people.

She realizes all of this, yet something was keeping her from engaging.

One day we were taking about my business and she blurted, "*I really like these products. I have the time. I think I would like to do this and I could use the extra income. But I just don't know what to say when people start asking me questions …I get really uncomfortable.*"

I thought, "Darlene uncomfortable? Really?"

After a bit of discussion she asked me if there were any "scripts" she could learn in case someone asked her a question like, "*Is this one of those pyramids?*"

By the way, the statement, "*I just don't know what to say when people start asking me questions,*" is a form of an objection. And the definition of an objection in the context of this book is any verbal challenge, question, concern, fear or belief that is causing a person to say no (or delay saying yes) to your product, service or opportunity.

I asked her to give me a few more examples of questions she was worried about.

"What if they tell me the product is too expensive? Then what do I say? What if they tell me only a few people at the top make money? How about that?"

After some thought I realized that while I was typically comfortable responding to most people's questions or objections, most of what I'd learned, practiced and taught over the years wasn't written down on paper.

I started writing with the idea of helping Darlene (or anyone) learn a few scripts that could help them better manage objections or questions. However, I realized after thinking about it more carefully that the scripts didn't hold the power. The scripts helped, but weren't the entire answer.

The effective power was in the "conversational model" I was using, along with important communication principles, a model I now call: the **Ultimate Power Prospecting Formula**.

I firmly believe that anyone – with a little practice and a simple system to follow – can learn to invite, present, follow up, manage objections and be more effective with their prospects.

Taking The Elephant For A Walk

After nearly 25 years in the direct selling/network marketing industry, I'm convinced there are three main reasons that well-intentioned people fail:

1. Not learning, or using a system for creating customers and/or distributors

2. Failure to take consistent action

3. Quitting too soon

Of course there are other reasons people fail:

Choosing the wrong products (not consumable, not unique, poor value proposition).

Choosing the wrong company (poor executive leadership, inadequate capital) and so on.

And what about those people who never get started in the first place? What about people who have a real need and desire for extra income, who would love to own their own business, but perhaps don't have the start-up capital or an idea of how or what to do next?

Why not consider network marketing?

Some people are afraid of starting a network marketing business because they know on some level that in order to be successful, they'll have to engage in a conversation with a friend, relative or stranger.

Some will say, "I don't want to look stupid, be embarrassed or feel rejected." Or, rather than admit it they protest, "I just don't want to sell," or say, "Network marketing doesn't work for the average person."

The standard industry response to this is, (and I groan when I hear it or see it in print) "You don't have to sell …just share the products or the opportunity."

Or worse, "Don't worry, this product sells itself."

Please allow me to apologize now, because I used to say this myself – until I learned it simply wasn't true.

The elephant in the room – the one that many networkers don't want to recognize or admit to – the "elephant we are going to take for a walk" is the question of selling….

That is, in order to be successful, do network marketers really have to learn to sell?

In my experience the answer is YES! In order to be successful, you will HAVE to learn to sell. Or you will have to be very good at recruiting others to do all the selling for you.

See the problem? You still have to sell others on that idea.

But there's GREAT news. You can easily learn, and teach others, a conversational model of selling that is much different from what most people mean when they say or describe "selling."

You can prospect successfully by learning a communications model that utilizes more natural "intentional conversations." This is an *authentic* method of communicating that creates clarity and direction – and anyone, with just a little practice, can easily learn the model.

Once you are familiar with the principles and concepts you can expect most of your prospecting, promoting, networking and "people communications" to improve greatly. You will have learned to "influence people with integrity" and with less wasted energy and angst.

My Mission

My mission with this book is to make it easier for you to speak with your prospects by providing you with a system that makes prospecting simple, uncomplicated and more productive.

In the context of network marketing, being more productive would mean accelerating the sales of your product or service; increasing the number of people that want to join your team;

reducing the time it takes to train people so they become more productive, and knowing when you are likely wasting your time with people.

Objections Handled will help you understand the principles and acquire the necessary communication skills so you can enjoy the process of turning prospects into willing customers or into willing members of your sales team.

Let's be realistic. When you don't enjoy doing something you have less energy and find reasons not to do it. You lose forward momentum. You make excuses for your lack of results.

On the other hand, when you acquire new skills and become good at something, you naturally tend do it more often. This gives you even more energy, and that energy builds naturally to create positive forward momentum.

Imagine This

Imagine feeling more relaxed and focused when prospecting. Imagine the feeling of satisfaction knowing you have the skills to help people take actions that were appropriate to their needs, and that you are very, very good at it.

While this book focuses on showing you how to effortlessly handle objections, you will also learn the **Power Prospecting Formula**, a simple "principle-based communications model" that will help supercharge your prospecting efforts.

What You Will Learn

- The *mindset* you *must have* for effective prospecting
- What people *really* want to hear
- How to effectively introduce your product or opportunity
- How to create conversations for instant rapport
- How to use conversations to qualify people
- How to tactfully discover people's needs

- How to offer a "needs-based" invitation
- How to clarify, diffuse, redirect and manage objections
- How to clarify next steps and focus your follow-up
- Techniques that can make your communications sizzle

If you are willing to take a little time to learn the art of "intentional conversations" and to elevate the quality of your communications by listening carefully and asking better questions, you can truly find opportunities to help others and add value to their lives.

Adding value to people's lives is what it's all about. It can be very rewarding –both emotionally and financially – and more importantly, your network marketing business will be positioned to flourish!

CHAPTER ONE

Adopting The Master Prospector's Mindset

"Intentions Rule The Earth"
– Oprah Winfrey

Objections Handled contains a collection of tools in the form of principles, concepts, insights, scripts and sample conversations to help you learn a system for handling objections as well as a "prospecting communications model" I call the "Power Prospecting Formula."

What's more important than the tools themselves is how you intend to use them, or your underlying intention.

Clarity of intention is an important concept. It will help you zero in on a *mindset* that will create better prospecting communications, which really means better people communications.

One definition of an intention is an "aim" or a "purpose." An intention is not a goal as much as it is a constant direction. When you are clear about your intentions, your conversations seem to flow – you're "on purpose."

The most important intention you can have; the one you *must have* to ensure you are positioned to become an extraordinary prospector and network marketer, is to have the intention to help people.

If you focus on using your skills for any intention other than this, my best guess is that you will struggle, if not fail.

Of course it's valuable to have personal dreams, goals, sales targets and the things you want to acquire or to achieve. Millions of network marketers have realized their personal, financial, lifestyle and time-freedom goals in this wonderful industry.

However, the reason most successful networkers accomplished what they wanted is because they had a clear intention to help others improve their lives.

The Physiology of Intention

In my opinion, this is what Oprah means when she says, *"...intentions rule the earth."*

(I happen to be an Oprah fan. What other self-made billionaire can you think of who has met, interviewed, befriended and experienced more successful people than Oprah Winfrey?)

Intentions manifest physically. In other words, your intentions create (or will eventually create) a physical form or outcome. Sooner or later your intentions are revealed in what you say or don't say; what you do or don't do; what you have or don't have; how you make others feel – good, bad, indifferent, excited, angry, hopeful, etc. Your intentions manifest themselves in what happens to you and for you – your outcomes.

While this may seem a bit metaphysical to you, believe it or not, on some level most people can "read" your intentions. For example, if your main intention is to make lots of money selling products, most people will read your intention and you will experience a higher level of resistance.

It's not that there's anything wrong with the intention of selling gobs of product or recruiting lots of people. It's more a question of "match up." Does what you're doing match up with people's true needs and does it improve their lives?

Beware Your Intention. Your Audience Knows

In earlier years, my business was managing the careers of musicians and entertainers. This gave me the opportunity to observe, critique and coach thousands of live performances.

One of the interesting "performance physiologies" I noticed, and attempted to coach, was an entertainer's underlying intention. The performer usually revealed his or her self by landing in one of two general camps of intention.

Camp One: "Look at me audience! Aren't I great?"

Camp Two: "Look at you audience! I'm here to help you feel great!"

Camp One is memorialized by a Fred Allen quip about an entertainer no one had heard from in years. Someone asked him, "Whatever happened to so and so?"

Fred responded, "The last time I saw him he was walking down lover's lane holding his own hand!"

So what does this have to do with prospecting and network marketing?

Simply this: Beware your intentions – your audience knows!

How To Be Unstoppable

If your main intention is to discover what others need, want or don't want, so that you can add value to their lives by providing your product or service, then you will find people who are eager to buy what you have. You will experience little or no resistance.

Some psychologists tell us that one of the best ways to read your true intentions is by looking at your results. For some of us this is worth reflecting on for a moment.

If your intention is to improve your prospecting (connecting, inviting, qualifying, handling objections, etc.) so you can help more people achieve what they need and desire, you will be an unstoppable network marketer.

"Most People Are Silently Begging To Be Led"

Author and marketing genius, Jay Abraham, continually reminds his clients and readers, "*Most people are silently begging to be led.*"

Here's what he means: In order to be in the best position to help people (prospects, clients, team members or anyone else you hope to influence) you must be willing to learn and understand their true needs.

This is the part where to support your intentions you have to be willing (and able) to take the lead in conversations. This is where you begin to put your intentions into action!

You must be willing to ethically and appropriately "lead" the communication by asking thoughtful questions in order to understand and solve people's concerns.

The good news is that most people are looking for a highly capable person to take the lead.

That's where you come in.

People are begging to be led by someone who can show them a better path; someone who has their best interests at heart. Taking the lead is a key to prospecting communications and an important key to network marketing success.

One of the very best ways to take the lead is by listening and asking quality questions. Help people discover, articulate and clarify what they want, need and desire. Often what they want is also what you want.

Everybody wins!

The Change of Focus Strategy

When prospecting you must make a simple strategy change –
an adjustment in focus, from "me" to "you." You do this by
acquiring the ability to *always* put the prospect's needs ahead
of your own.

This simple strategy will turn your prospects into customers or
team members; and some of these into friends for life. It will
strengthen your passion and connection to everyone with
whom you associate.

It is perhaps one of the most powerful business,
communication and life strategies you can employ.

Listen More. Talk Less. Ask Questions

In order to become more effective you will want to learn to
listen more and talk less. One suggestion is to listen about
80% and talk about 20%. It's not an exact science or rule, but
maybe asking yourself the following will help:

"Whom would I like to lead the conversation?"

The person asking the questions is always the person
controlling (and leading) the conversation. If you're busy
answering someone else's questions, they are in control,
which means they are leading the conversation. Just to be
clear, you are not trying to control the person, just the positive
direction of the conversation.

When you're having a prospecting conversation, two things
should be happening: You listening carefully and you asking
questions. Hint: The more you listen, the better your questions
and the more effective you will be.

Fall In Love With The Right Thing

You are enriched in direct proportion to the value you bring to your market. Your market is people. People have questions and issues and concerns they sometimes can't even verbalize. This is where you come in and provide value.

The quality of your questions determines the quality of your answers. Quality answers create more clarity. The significance of helping people find the right words is worth a fortune!

Many people are out of focus. If you can help them focus, they can gain clarity; and clarity creates certainty. Certainty engenders trust, and when people trust they tend to take action.

What do they want? Where are they hurting? What are they not getting? What do they need that they're not expressing openly or publicly? What are they not getting from someone else? In which area of their lives are they not satisfied?

My friend and super-successful network marketer, Tom Alkazin calls this, "being needs aware."

Everything in life is about the value and contribution you make. You have to love your market and be connected with your market. And your market is people. Fall in love with helping people.

Sell What People Are Buying

It's a less trusting, less "marketing friendly" world. Most people don't trust the system. They feel they're being taken for a ride. Often they're right. They suspect there may be better alternatives that no one is telling them about. People believe they're not being told the whole truth. They "don't know what they don't know."

When people feel this way, they end up thinking, "This is not for me."

YOUR job is to prove that you understand them and you're not just paying lip service.

Create a bridge of understanding. Position yourself to be their "3-D glasses." Help them see what they're not seeing.

Put into words *how* what you're offering helps them achieve their goals or solves their problems. Your ability to communicate effectively and influence people in a positive direction is *your currency*!

Understand that attention is becoming the scarcest commodity in today's world, so you have to reward people's attention – you have to provide value sooner. How do you do this?

Give people your *attention*. Listen!

Sell *empathy, attention, connectedness, leadership*, and *clarity*! Sell solutions that solve people's problems.

This is what people are buying.

Risking Yourself

It's interesting to note that when most people think of taking risks, what they're thinking of is risking money. But many of the risks people fail to take – and the possible rewards they miss – actually cost nothing.

These risks are personal.

We meet an energetic, upbeat service person while shopping and we fail to engage them. We're afraid. We have a friend we believe could benefit from our product or opportunity and we're worried about what they might think. We don't make the call.

We don't put ourselves "out there."

In her book, *Pathfinders*, researcher Gail Sheehy revealed one of the more surprising common behaviors of "truly centered people." These were people who enjoyed an enormous internal sense of accomplishment and well-being.

What was the common behavior?

They had pushed themselves to take personal risks!

Understand: Taking risks doesn't always mean risking your money. Sometimes it simply means risking *yourself* a little.

Selling your product, service or opportunity involves taking personal risks. You can seem pushy. People may not return your calls. People are sometimes rude. You can be rejected. (Actually, what you offer will be rejected at times). Rejection can sting. You run the risk of feeling emotionally drained.

The late business philosopher, Jim Rohn, reported the most common emotion he uncovered when coaching unfulfilled people was a feeling of regret. The sense that they had somehow done less than they were capable of. And as they looked back on their lives they asked, "Why didn't I just go for it?"

The rewards, when you find a way to "push through" can be enormously positive – sometimes staggering.

A few years ago I had the opportunity to interview Todd Smith, master network marketer and author of two outstanding books, *The Cycle of Duplication*, and *Little Things Matter*. I asked Todd if there was any advice he could offer the audience.

His response: "*Yes.* One of the keys to success is having the discipline to do, what you know you should do, even when you don't feel like doing it." (Todd leaned strongly on the "*...you know*" in his answer.)

I think we all know what "...*Do what you know you should do*," means: Have intentional conversations, talk to people, engage them, prospect, promote, make the call, connect, invite someone to take a look at what you have to offer. Take a few risks.

Network marketing is simple; it's mostly about creating conversations, developing relationships and helping people. If I had to summarize what it is we really do in just a few words, I would offer this description:

Make a friend. Meet their friends. Risk yourself.

Summarizing The Master Prospector's Mindset

- Have the true intention to help people.
- Be willing to take the lead in conversations.
- Have an external focus: "It's not about me, it's about you."
- Fall in love with the right thing: Helping people.
- Be "needs aware."
- Listen more. Talk less. Ask questions.
- Sell what people are buying: Connectedness; Attention; Leadership; Empathy; Clarity.

Seek first to understand, then be understood.

STEVEN COVEY

CHAPTER TWO

The Ultimate Power Prospecting Formula

One of the single most important business questions you can ask yourself is: "What are the 10-20% of the activities that will create 80-90% of the results in my network marketing business?"

Where should I focus? What activity will give me the greatest return on my efforts?

What should I be really good at?

The answer is PROSPECTING!

The definition of prospecting is: To look for; to investigate; to examine and to probe for; with the expectation or a vision of the outcome.

The desired outcome in network marketing is to encourage the adoption of or sale of a product, service or an opportunity. In other words, *prospecting is everything you do to acquire a new customer or create a new team member*.

Are there other activities that can positively impact the growth of your network marketing business? Yes – but let's be clear – no single activity will offer a greater return on your personal time invested than prospecting.

Your ability to prospect effectively can make or break your network marketing business – it is perhaps the greatest predictor of your future success.

The **Ultimate Power Prospecting Formula** is made up of several activities or steps. If prospecting were a great cake recipe, these would be the ingredients:

(1) CONNECT
(2) QUALIFY
(3) INVITE
(4) INTRODUCE
(5) MANAGE OBJECTIONS
(6) CLOSE TO ACTION
(7) FOLLOW UP

While these seven activities or steps can be distinct, they often blend seamlessly into one another. For example, you can *connect* and build rapport with someone and in the same conversation begin to *qualify* him or her.

In the next moment you may *invite* them to review your business (or sample a product) and if the timing is right you may hand them a tool to introduce the business. At any point along the way you may find yourself *managing objections* and *closing to action* or suggesting next steps.

Author's message: If you are more of a visual or auditory learner, let me suggest that after reading this chapter, you may also want to go to www.montetaylor.com/freestuff *where you can view the free streaming videos I've created to help you learn and internalize the* **Power Prospecting** *steps.*

For clarity, let's define and expand on the seven activities that make up prospecting:

1. Connecting – To create rapport; a relationship of harmony and mutual understanding; a close connection or trust marked by a feeling of affinity, closeness, or kinship.

2. Qualifying – To prove capable or fit; meet requirements of; to make eligible for or to determine if something or someone is suitable.

3. Inviting – To welcome, suggest, entice, to go after, to ask someone to do something or request to participate.

4. Introducing – To present; to make known or to bring before the public; to offer for observation, examination or consideration; to show or display.

5. Managing Objections – To successfully handle, answer, redirect, overcome or respond to a prospect's doubts, opposition, concerns or questions.

6. Closing To Action – To conclude, complete. To reach an agreement; come to terms.

7. Following Up – To finish to completion; follow through on. To increase the effectiveness or enhance the success of by further action.

Two Essential Supporting Skills

There are two essential skills that empower all successful prospecting:

1. Your ability to LISTEN.

2. Your ability to ask (quality) QUESTIONS.

The importance of careful LISTENING is common knowledge to most people, but not necessarily common practice. Most people don't listen with the intent to understand but with the intent to reply. Most people are busy speaking or preparing to speak.

Don't be like *most* people – commit to being a "master communicator," a "professional prospector" who listens.

Once you develop the habit of careful listening, it will be much easier to develop the skill of asking quality questions and having "intentional conversations."

1. CONNECT – To create rapport, a relationship of harmony and mutual understanding; a close connection or trust marked by a feeling of affinity, closeness, or kinship.

The Cocktail Party "Take Away"

Let's assume you're at a cocktail party. It's loud and you're listening to someone speak. Suddenly you hear your name mentioned in another conversation a few feet away. What happens (for most of us) is that you will quickly tune into the "you" conversation and tune out the "not about you" conversation. It's just human nature.

Like most people, you can only listen to and be interested in one conversation at a time and the ONE that will immediately grab your attention is *any conversation about YOU.*

What you can learn from the "The Cocktail Party Take Away" is that dozens of conversations (both internal and external) are going on around people at any given moment.

So … if you want to quickly capture someone's attention (and "connect") then engage the person in conversation that focuses directly on him or her.

"Jane, Vicki tells me you're one of the most gifted teachers she knows. Would you mind telling me what made you decide to become a teacher?"

(Whenever possible, pay the person a sincere compliment and follow up with a question that shows an interest in learning more about them!)

"Bill, I understand you are an expert in social media. I'd love to hear how you learned so much about it. Would you tell me more?"

"Seek first to understand then be understood" – *Steven Covey*

Connecting by focusing on listening and understanding people is not a technique – **it's a principle** – and one of Steven Covey's, *7 Habit's of Highly Effective People.*

Network marketing relies on relationship building; connecting and creating rapport is absolutely essential! From the moment you encounter a prospect on the phone or in person, you must always begin by first seeking to build rapport and connect.

The message you want to send is: *"You are a very interesting person. I'd like to get to know you better."*

Knowing, trusting and liking are attributes of rapport. Let's get to know each other better. Over time, perhaps we can learn to trust and like each other.

Connecting Questions

Here are a few connecting questions (and statements) to help you comfortably open or bridge conversations. They can also help keep you from sounding like the "Inquisitor General" when you're getting to know a person better.

Remember, you're trying to connect, and if the timing is right, learn how you may be able to help someone with your product, service or business opportunity.

"I'm wondering…"

"I'm curious…"

"Would you be willing…?"

"Please tell me about…"

"I'm interested…"

"I'm wondering if you'd tell me more about yourself."

"I'm wondering what specifically you meant by, FILL IN THE BLANK?" (Something they've said that you would like them to expand upon or clarify).

"I'm curious about, FILL IN THE BLANK (their job, their car, their smile, something they said, something they're wearing).

"I'm curious …what did you like best about, FILL IN THE BLANK?"

"Please tell me more about your job, it sounds interesting." Or, *"Please tell me what projects you're working on that you're excited about."*

"Would you be willing to tell me the story about how you and Mary met?"

Connecting and building rapport is not just the first step in prospecting; it is an essential part of any communication. Rapport means a relationship of harmony, accord or affinity.

How do you know when you have it? Some people describe rapport as a positive feeling; a shared sense of comfort and understanding; a general lifting of mutual energies and spirits.

Rapport is like money, its value increases dramatically when you do not have it and when you do have it opportunities seem to abound.

How can you quickly connect and gain rapport?

Listen carefully to people! Use questions to build a bridge of trust and understanding. Be interested in learning about them, their values and their needs. Look for opportunities to help people gain positive outcomes with your products or opportunity; but make sure helping people is your highest intention.

A Simple Way To Connect With People

There's no better way to quickly connect and begin building rapport than by being enthusiastic when you first greet someone. You can do this by sending a clear message with your voice, tone and attitude, that you are absolutely, genuinely delighted to meet them; or if you've already met, you are pleased to see them again.

Almost everyone can think of someone in his or her life; a favorite aunt, uncle, friend, sibling or someone who always seemed REALLY glad to see you. I'm not suggesting you gush or over-express yourself – just be aware. Don't underestimate how the way you first greet someone has the power to set a positive tone and have a favorable impact.

Avoiding The "I'm Interesting" Trap

There's one trap we all have to watch out for, and that's making the mistake of redirecting the conversational focus and making it about you rather than the prospect.

For example, if someone mentions that they are from Atlanta, Georgia. You might comment, "*Oh, wonderful. I was born and raised there!*" (So far so good …you're connecting …you have some things in common to share.)

Then you make the mistake of continuing on and tell them about the neighborhood you grew up in, the high school you graduated from in Atlanta, your first job there, your upcoming reunion, …blah, blah, blah. You just made it all about YOU.

You've fallen in to the trap of trying to connect by *being interesting* rather than by *being interested*. You took the focus off the prospect and put it back on you.

Of course it's important to share your connecting values and interests, but make sure you are communicating your interest in THEM rather than attempting to show them how interesting YOU are.

Here's an example of responding to connect and create rapport, but keeping the conversational focus on the prospect. The secret is to respond and then follow your response with a question.

Prospect: *"I just moved here from Atlanta."*

You: *"Oh, wonderful. I was born and raised in Atlanta and still have many friends in the area. Did you enjoy living there? ...What brought you here? ...Do you still have family there?"*

Focus on being interested – not interesting. Don't worry. If you are genuinely interested in people they'll find you VERY interesting!

Important take away: The very first step in "power prospecting" is to connect and create rapport. Without it no communication will ever be entirely successful.

2. QUALIFY – To prove capable or fit; meet requirements of; to make eligible for or to determine if something or someone is suitable.

When most people think of qualifying, they think of it as finding out if people have enough money or credit to purchase a product or service.

As a Power Prospector, you want to think of qualifying as discovering or identifying a person's needs, wants or desires so you can decide:

1. If you want to invite that person to look at or review your business or product.

2. How best to invite that person to look at or review your business or product.

Many of the same questions you use to connect and build rapport will also provide valuable information to help you qualify the person's need.

Qualifying Questions are the answer to determining need:

"I'm wondering…"

"I'm curious…"

"Would you be willing...?"

"Tell me about…"

"Would you mind if I asked you a question about…?"

Qualifying questions for business and financial health:

"Bill, how are things going with your job?"

"Jane, how is the economy affecting your business?"

"How are things going in your life?

How are you getting along?"

"Do you ever think about protecting yourself with a Plan B?"

Qualifying questions for health and well being:

"How do you keep your energy levels up?"

"What kind of things do you do to prevent disease?"

"How do you make sure your children (or family) get all the nutrients they need?"

"On a scale of one to ten, Mary, how important is your health?"

"Bill, what are you doing to reduce stress and stay healthy?"

Qualifying questions for lifestyle:

"How does your family decide where to vacation?"

"When is the last time you and your wife took a great vacation together?"

"Do you worry about what would happen to your family if you were unable to work?"

"Do you ever feel like you don't have enough time to accomplish what you want?"

Once you learn a person is 'less than satisfied' with something in their business or personal life, you are positioned to deliver an invitation that addresses their need, desire or problem and offer possible solutions.

The Difference Between Suspects and Prospects

An important and timesaving question to ask yourself when prospecting: "Is the person I'm speaking with a PROSPECT …or in reality just a SUSPECT?"

Suspects *are not* qualified – Prospects *are* qualified

How do you know which is which?

Qualify them with questions!

Suspect: Someone you haven't qualified in terms of a need or desire. You have little or no idea if they might want or need what you have to offer. You may think they need it but you haven't confirmed that by asking questions. Because you haven't determined their need you are not positioned to effectively invite them to review what you have to offer.

Prospect: A person you have qualified. This person has shared enough information with you for you to determine that they do indeed qualify for an invitation to review what you have to offer.

Important take away: Qualifying is all about discovering or identifying a person's needs so you can decide the best way to invite the person to review your product, opportunity or both. Master prospectors know that qualifying is vital to their overall success and can dramatically save them time and wasted energy.

3. INVITE – To welcome, suggest, entice; to go after; to ask someone to do something or request to participate.

The next step is to INVITE. There are three main objectives of your invitation.

1. To connect your invitation to the prospect's pain, needs, wants or desires in a way that suggests or offers a possible solution.

2. To arouse interest and curiosity so they will want to learn about your product or business as soon as possible.

3. To gain a firm commitment (an agreed-upon date or time) for a person to meet with you or review any other tool you are providing as an introductory overview.

Once you are confident asking qualifying and inviting questions you can often qualify and invite in the same conversation. In the example below, you've started with a sincere greeting followed by a compliment and a question. Since the prospect gave you an opening (a need) you can proceed directly to an invitation.

Reminder: There is little or no chance of a positive interaction without rapport. Always begin with a "friendly hello" and a few sincere questions. Find ways to pay a sincere compliment. If you share genuine respect or admiration for the person, go ahead and tell them why, but *be authentic*.

"Hi Marc, how are you?"

Marc: *"Great."*

"Are you still working at Home Depot?"

Marc: *"Yes, I'm still working there."*

"I've always noticed what a hard worker you are. Do you still enjoy it?"

Marc: *"I do, but all the weekend hours are really starting to get me down. I work more weekends than I'd like …but I really don't have any choice."*

"I know how difficult it must be always having to work on weekends…"

(So far you've connected and qualified Marc by discovering a possible area of need; he's always working on weekends. Now you can go directly into your invitation).

Remember: Whenever possible, tie your invitation to the person's *need*.

The Business Invitation

"Marc, I have a very interesting business idea that may help solve your problem. Would you be open to seeing something on it or are you completely satisfied with how you're doing?"

"Is your schedule open for coffee or to get together at my house this week?"

*"The reason I'm asking is I've discovered a concept that has tremendous income potential and may resolve… (*The issue*) Would you be open to taking a look or are you completely satisfied now?"*

Or:

"I've been thinking about our conversation last week …we've been friends for some time, but never really discussed business. Would you mind if we did?"

"I've recently seen an online presentation I think you'll benefit from seeing. Are you open to a business idea you and I could do together?"

"I've been thinking of you because I've always admired (your energy, enthusiasm, work ethic, willingness to help people, etc.).

"Would you be open to talking about how we might work together on an interesting business idea, or are you completely satisfied with everything you're doing?"

The "Resolve A Need" Invitation

"I've been thinking about our last conversation (fill in the need …such as they said they never have free time) *and I believe I have a possible solution. Would you be open to hearing about it?"*
"Is your schedule open for coffee or to get together at my house this week?

"The reason I'm asking is when we spoke last time, you mentioned (fill in the pain, problem or financial need). *I've discovered a concept that has tremendous income potential."*
"Would you be open to taking a look, or are you completely satisfied now?"

"The last time we spoke you shared how much the economy is hurting your business. There's an online movie I think you'd benefit from seeing. Do you have Internet access?"

"Jane, you told us several times how painful it's been for you to miss so many of your children's after school and sports events because of your work. I believe I have a possible solution. Would you be open to getting together to hear about it?"

"Dave, I know how challenging your work has been this year. If there were a business you could start part-time from home that could later replace your full-time income, would that be something you'd like to know more about?"

The Discovery Invitation

"Bill, how are things going with your job?"

"Jane, how is the economy affecting your business?"

"How are things going in your life? How are you getting along these days?"

If after learning that they are less than satisfied with their job, or their lifestyle is being negatively impacted, you can ask them to elaborate or simply ask,

"Would you be open to looking at a business concept that has serious financial potential."?

"Let me ask you off the record. If there were a business you could start part-time that could later replace your full-time income, would that be of interest to you?"

"Lee, if I could show you a profitable part-time business that would allow you to make extra money while the kids are in school, would you want to hear about it?"

Social Media Invitations

Mass invitations to your 'warm market' are impersonal and have never been an effective way to invite people to learn about your business or product. Direct personal messages are always the best. If you're going to use Facebook, for example, use it only to schedule an appointment to speak on the phone or in person.

"Hi Bill. Hope this note finds you doing well. I have something I'd like to discuss with you. Would you be available tomorrow between 3-5 or Tuesday AM between 10-12? Let me know the number you want me to call. Looking forward to speaking with you."

"Mary, can we speak in the next day or so? Based on your post a few weeks ago I have an idea I want to run by you. Please send me a time that works for you."

"Hi Dave. You mentioned in one of your posts that you've been having some health challenges lately. I don't want to be nosy or intrude, but would you be open to some ideas? If so, let me know a time we could speak and I'll fill you in."

As you meet people each day, ask questions about their jobs or lives. When they respond, listen carefully to see if you can identify a need, a concern or pain that your business or product could help resolve.

Important take away: If you are "needs aware" and have invested the time to learn about the challenges a person is experiencing, you are positioned to offer an effective invitation to have them review your product, service or business opportunity.

4. INTRODUCE – To present; to make known or to bring before the public; to offer for observation, examination or consideration; to show or display

Once you have taken your prospect through the CONNECTING, QUALIFYING and INVITING steps, you are ready for one of the easiest and most enjoyable steps; and that is introducing your product or opportunity.

The key to INTRODUCING is to identify one or more of your company's professional tools and allow the tool to do the work!

One of the most important things to remember with professional tools is that *you are the messenger, not the message* – think of yourself as the 30-second commercial promoting the upcoming show or movie.

Here are some of the most popular ways to present and introduce your product or business to others using professionally produced tools:

- Audio CD's
- DVD's
- Streaming Media (Audio or Video)
- Your corporate website
- Pre-recorded introductory conference/presentation calls
- Printed materials such as retail catalogs, brochures, PowerPoint presentations, and company branded magazines and other print media.

Using professionally produced tools has several advantages:

- Using tools is more duplicable – anyone can hand out a tool or direct a prospect to a streaming audio or video link on the Internet. Not everyone can offer a compelling presentation, especially when they are new to the business.

- It's time-efficient – you can use the tools to help you sift and sort through people who are truly interested. People can review the tool when it's convenient. It's easier for many people to review a tool than it is to attend a presentation.

- A professionally produced tool is often more credible than a personal presentation – and more consistent as well.

- A person can review the introductory tool multiple times – each time they can learn more or build more belief in what you're offering

- Most people are more comfortable offering a professional tool than they are making a presentation

INTRODUCE via "Personal Presentations."

- One-on-One Introductions – this is when you meet personally with a prospect at your home, a coffee shop or any other location that is generally free of distractions. You give your prospect a private overview of your product or opportunity and perhaps support your presentation with professionally produced print media.

- Two-on-One Introductions – this is when you and one of your up line business partners meet with a prospect in a suitable location or via a conference call. This gives you the opportunity to have an experienced third-party handle the presentation, plus it allows you to listen in and learn *how* to introduce the business. (To download my free report/training, "*Checklist, Tips and Sample Scripts for Outrageously Successful 3-Way Conference Calls,*" go to www.montetaylor.com/freestuff)

- Private Business Mixers – This is an opportunity to introduce your business to a small group, perhaps in your home, a country club, a meeting room or any other suitable location. You and your up line partner can handle the presentation to your guests and whenever possible support the presentation with professionally produced print or media tools.

- Large Group Presentations - These are another type of in-person introductory presentation that generally takes place in a hotel or a private banquet room at a country club or restaurant. Typically these presentations feature one or more top distributors or company executives who introduce the products and business opportunities. Large group presentations are more effective for providing information to people who have already been introduced through a tool or personal presentations. They are NOT recommended as a first introduction.

The Advantages of Personal Introductions

1. Gives the presenter the opportunity to customize the introduction for the audience.

2. Creates an opportunity to have the person's or the audience's undivided attention for the length of the presentation and eliminate outside distractions.

3. Creates an opportunity for the person or audience to interact and ask questions after the presentation, and perhaps sample products.

Introductory Presentation Questions

Here are some questions you can ask a prospect (or the members of your audience) to think about during a presentation. In some cases you may be asking the audience to consider or raise their hand in response, but not necessarily answer out loud.

"Have you ever thought about how important it could be to create a "Plan B" just in case something happened to your current income or your job?"

"How many, if given a choice, would choose not to live under financial pressure?"

"Have you ever considered how you might be able to create a substantial secondary income stream with part-time effort?"

"What can you do today to create an economic home run?"

"Where are you going to plant your financial freedom flag?"

"What's your financial freedom number?" (See Chapter 11)

Post Introductory Questions
(After You Have Introduced Someone To Your Business)

Note: These are also "follow on" questions that will help lead you naturally to the next two steps in the Ultimate Power Prospecting formula: MANAGING OBJECTIONS (questions or concerns) and CLOSING TO NEXT STEPS

"What did you like best about what you saw or heard?"

"Do you see yourself as more of a product (or service) person, a business builder, or both?"

"What kind or residual cash flow would you like to create?"

"Would you like to make a little money or a lot?"

"Would you like to know the next steps?"

"Is there anything else you need to know before you consider joining our team?"

"On a scale of 1-10, with 1 being low, how would you rate your overall interest level after seeing the presentation?"

"Are you ready to get started?"

Important take away when introducing with a tool: Don't forget to be the messenger, not the message. Your job is to simply introduce the tool by creating interest and excitement and get the prospect's agreement to (1) review the tool and (2) provide you with their feedback or comments.

5. MANAGE OBJECTIONS – To successfully handle, answer, redirect, overcome or respond to a prospect's doubts, opposition, concerns or questions.

Perhaps the biggest challenge for most network marketers – the one that keeps many networkers from actively prospecting – is the fear of what to say and how to effectively respond to people's questions or objections.

One of the very first obstacles you have to overcome is your fear of addressing people's verbal challenges, issues and some times "energy -charged" questions.

- "I don't like to sell."
- "I don't want to have to talk people into buying anything."
- "Is this one of those pyramids?"
- "If this is a network marketing scheme, I'm not interested."
- "Oh, those pyramid things never work."
- "Those products cost too much."
- "I'm way too busy…I don't have any time."
- "Only a few people ever make any money."

By the way, these are simply beliefs or automatic scripts. Part of learning to manage objections is to understand that some of your prospect's fears, concerns or objections are legitimate and some are based on mistaken or misinformed beliefs.

It's important to remember that we live in a "belief-driven universe" – people's beliefs are people's beliefs. At times, no matter how hard you try, you may never be able to change another person's beliefs.

The only belief system you CAN control is your personal belief system. You must recognize and examine *your own beliefs* because *your* personal beliefs, including your beliefs about selling, network marketing and your beliefs about your skills greatly impact your ability to prospect successfully.

People's "automatic scripts," on the other hand, don't always represent their beliefs. Some people respond with scripts more or less reflexively. For example, no matter what the price of something, they'll respond with, "It's too expensive." Or ask them to do anything requiring some of their time and they'll respond routinely, "I'm too busy."

In a moment you'll learn about powerful "expanding questions" that can help you determine if you're dealing with a belief, an automatic script, or a real objection.

I Strenuously Object!

An objection is something that a person (a prospect) is opposed to; in conflict with; resistant to or against. Are you dealing with fears, mistaken beliefs, concerns or just preferences?

A person could be resistant to marriage, for example, or totally against eating red meat. They could like or dislike broccoli. They may prefer soup to salad.

Understanding if they are "resistant" or "totally against" is one of your first objectives and will help you recognize how strong a position a person is going to take on the subject. Are they taking a position at all? Are they tossing out an automatic script? Do they just want to be heard? What do they want to express?

Objections can come from their past experiences, doubts about themselves or from something they've read or heard and perhaps misunderstood.

One of your jobs is to accept the role of "gentle detective" and to keep asking questions until you understand what a person needs, wants or doesn't want. It's a blend of art and science.

Your best tools are a *curious mind*, *great questions* and a willingness and *intention to help people*.

Two Kinds of Objections

There are two basic kinds of objections: Expressed and unexpressed.

1. Expressed objections are when a prospect says something like, "I don't like selling." or "This product seems too expensive." Sometimes what they express isn't clear; so you'll have to probe for clarity and understanding.

2. Unexpressed objections are trickier. When a prospect is vague, uncommunicative, won't return your call or simply shows no interest, it can signal that they have an objection but won't tell you about it. Sometimes it's a feeling, or perhaps a fear, that they can't or won't articulate. It's unexpressed. On the other hand, it just may be that *it's not a good time to introduce anything new to their life.*

In the next chapters I will show you come strategies that will help you bring unexpressed objections to the surface so you can handle them. However, you will have to decide for yourself how much time you're willing to spend on helping prospects express their unexpressed objections.

Remember, the goal is to help you *ethically* solve the concern so you can help them make a decision to buy, purchase, engage or get involved, ONLY if that's what they need.

Once you are proficient at "MANAGING OBJECTIONS," the rest of the steps in the Ultimate Power Prospecting Formula begin to fall into place and the communications process begins to flow.

If you can learn this simple system of "communication flow" to handle your prospect's objections, you've taken one of the most important steps towards becoming a power prospector and expert communicator. You can be a leader that people want to be around, follow and do business with.

Your Voice Is Unique

Even though you're following a system and perhaps borrowing the scripts – don't forget to be yourself. You are unique. No one will have your exact style of communicating, your exact words, or have your voice or style.

Always keep your intention to help people at the forefront of your mind. Of course you want new customers or team members in your business, but what's important is if what you're providing adds value to people's lives and serves them.

Listen/Feel/Felt/Found/Question

This is your first system for managing objections: Listen/Feel/Felt/Found/Question is a very simple SYSTEM of "communication flow" that will help you become much more effective at responding to people's objections.

Your very first objective is to *listen carefully* to whatever they have to say before you do anything else. Don't forget, careful listening is an important fundamental success principle of the system.

Listening carefully is as important to the Ultimate Power Prospecting Formula as oxygen is to breathing.

People want to be respected. People want to be acknowledged. You can accomplish both by listening carefully as someone is speaking, expressing a concern or asking a question.

Don't just listen just with your ears. Listen with your eyes, your face and your body language. Pay attention to people's body language.

Remember the times when someone was just pretending to listen to you? We've all had experiences when we realize someone is not truly listening to what we are saying. They are fiddling with their cell phone or texting ...or you can literally feel them preparing to jump in with a response.

When someone isn't "tuned in" to you when you're speaking or communicating, you don't feel respected or acknowledged. There is little or no opportunity for connection or rapport.

There are professionals who earn six and seven figure incomes because they have developed high level listening skills. Their core competency is listening. Many will tell you they spend the vast majority of their time simply listening carefully and attentively before responding or advising people.

Have you ever noticed how supported and respected you feel when the person you are speaking with is quiet, tuned in, aware and very intent on learning about whatever it is you want to communicate?

Don't commit the sin of being distracted when others are speaking to you.

So first: LISTEN intently to the objection, whether it's a fear, concern, question or belief.

Listen/Feel/Felt/Found/Question

Next, acknowledge their objection. Acknowledge their absolute right to express a concern and offer their point of view.

You can do this by thanking them for sharing their objection, confirming your understanding of the objection and letting them know (if it's true) that you or others have had the same or similar concerns.

Fundamentally, it's about letting them know you appreciate their point of view. You don't have to agree with it, but you absolutely respect and value their right to voice it.

Here are some examples

Prospect: *"I just don't think I could sell. I'm very uncomfortable selling."*

You: *"Mary, I'm so glad you brought this up. A lot of people **feel** the same way...they're just not comfortable with what seems like selling at first. Actually, I **felt** the same way in the beginning...but what I **found** was, with the company's outstanding training, plus a few days of practice ...I learned I could easily talk to almost anyone about our products and the opportunity."*

Or:

You: *"Mary, you're right on. Thanks for mentioning this. I was surprised when I **found** out that many of the top performers in our company **felt** exactly the same way you do in the beginning. They weren't experienced and didn't **feel** they could be successful ...but what they **found** was, with the company's outstanding training, plus a few days of practice ...they could easily talk to most anyone about our products and the opportunity."*

So far you've (1) listened, (2) acknowledged how they feel, (3) validated their concern by pointing out that you and others felt the same way, (4) shared the positive information you and others found.

The next step is to *ask a question* to clarify that you've handled or answered their objection or concern, and if so, guide them to action steps or a tool – an event, training, book,

CD – or a person that addresses their needs, wants or concerns.

You (with a question): *"Mary, if you knew for sure that we can train anyone who's willing and coachable so they could be comfortable and effective in just a short time, would that address your concern? Would you be willing to come to our exclusive "learn to sell without selling" seminar next weekend so you can see first hand how great our training is for people like you and me?"*

Remember, you are not in a war of words. You are not trying to win a "battle of the minds." Don't pounce on your prospect or overwhelm them with your snappy comebacks or questions. Take your time, listen, and be thoughtful.

Remember too; part of what people are looking for is to see how *you* handle yourself. They want to find out if you're a leader they can follow, believe in and learn from.

When you begin to comfortably handle questions and objections you are putting yourself in a position to build a bridge or a relationship with that person. In the beginning you are their "thinking partner." If they join you, you may become true team members.

You are also qualifying your potential relationship with the prospect. You may decide after the "conversation," based on their current situation, needs or other factors, they're not right for your team.

Variation: Respond With A Question

A very effective strategy is to first respond (after listening) **with a question** that invites them to expand on their initial objection.

So: Listen/**Question**/Feel/Felt/Found/Question

Here's an example:

Prospect: *"So, is this one of those pyramid things?"* Or *"...is this network marketing?"*

You: *"Mary, good question. Would you mind if I asked you first, what's your experience with network marketing?*

Prospect: *I've just heard that a lot of people have a problem, and only a few people at the top do well." ...etc., etc.*

You: *"Mary, I know how you feel, and frankly I felt the same way in the beginning. But what I found was that what we really do is social marketing. It's a thriving industry with millions of good people sharing their passion for products and enjoying the success that came with owning their own business."*

You've responded and can now ask some questions:

"Mary, I have a DVD created by one of the top business minds in the world, sharing his independent research about our industry. Would you be willing to watch it in the next day or two so you can get some additional perspective?"

"I have a booklet (article, tape, brochure, video link) about the industry by the well know author _____. Would you be willing to review it in the next day or two and give me your feedback? I'm really interested in knowing what you like best about it.

Listen/Feel/Felt/Found/**Question**

Remember: At the end of any exchange, try to ask a question to confirm that you've adequately addressed their concern and then ask if the person is willing to take the next step.

You: *"Dave, I have this short book, The Business of the 21st Century, written by the well-known author Robert Kiyosaki. I'd love to get your opinion on it. Would you be willing to review it in the next two or three days and share your impressions with me?"*

You: *"Lucy, I agree how important it is that you have your own positive experience with our product in order for you to be excited. Lets get your order placed today. Or, "I have product ready for you to take home with you today, OK?"*

Your Question: *"Could I also suggest that you speak briefly with a few of my customers so you can gain some insights on how our product is helping others?"*

Now You Have Your First System For Managing Objections

Listen/Feel/Felt/Found/Question

Or,

Listen/Question/Feel/Felt/Found/Question

How do you decide which to use? Good question!

How much information do you need? How interested are you in getting to the heart of their concern? How much time do you have? What's your intuition telling you?

In the following chapters you'll learn some additional scripts that utilize the Listen/Question/Feel/Felt/Found/Question system. In addition I'll introduce a second system for Managing Objections called **AVVIS**, which is similar but a bit more robust.

You can easily learn both and will soon recognize opportunities to use one or the other, or both.

Important take away: Master prospectors don't "wing it" when someone asks a question or offers an objection. They've learned to follow a system.

Moreover, be authentic. Be interested in their point of view. Don't try to be clever. Immediately acknowledge a person's right to have concerns or questions.

Use your own expanding questions to gain clarity so you can handle people's apprehensions effectively, professionally, and with respect.

6. CLOSE TO ACTION (OR NEXT STEPS) – To conclude, complete. To reach an agreement; come to terms.

Closing has been compared to buttoning the last button of an overcoat. You've taken your prospect through the other steps of the prospecting communications system: CONNECTING, QUALIFYING, INVITING, INTRODUCING, AND MANAGING OBJECTIONS.

Once you've confirmed their needs, wants desires, fears or prejudices and have led them to discover how the benefits of your product, service or opportunity will make their life better – then it's easy to get to the last button.

Closing is about *clarity*. If you want clarity, ask questions. If you want to be a master prospector and skilled closer, ask even better questions.

Remember, closing is nothing more than "leading the communications" and helping people take appropriate next steps. Closing is about helping people clarify their thoughts and make decisions. Closing is not trying to convince people; which doesn't work and doesn't serve anyone's interests in the long term. Closing is about achieving clarity for you and for the prospect.

Here are some outstanding general questions you can ask following your introduction or after you've addressed initial objections. These questions can help you understand what a person is thinking or feeling and help draw them in to a conversation that clarifies issues or leads to decisions on the next steps.

"Peter, after everything you've seen so far, do you see yourself as more of a product person, a business builder, or both?"

"Robert, I'm eager to hear your impressions and feedback. What did you like best about the presentation?"

Asking for A Decision

If for example, after a 3-way call you feel the person is "generally positive" you could do a soft close by asking:

"Hey Bill, now that we seem to have covered most of the things you wanted to know about, would you like to know the next steps?"

"Jamie, based on all the information we've reviewed to this point, is there anything else you need to know before I explain how to get started?"

Hint: Be sure you're prepared to outline the next steps if they say, "Yes."

A slight variation is to summarize first, then close:

"Mary, you've asked some great questions, and with your experience (or personality, or positive energy, or "what you've shared," etc.) I really feel we could build a successful business together. I would truly enjoy working with you to help you achieve your goals.

The CLOSE: *"...Is there anything else you need to know OR are you ready to get started now?"*

46

If the person seems hesitant, or YOU are not sure about their level of interest, then below are questions that can help you get some clarity on what's holding them back.

Reluctance Closing Question

Sometimes people are hesitant and maybe they're not even sure why. Their concern or question is "unexpressed." They may not know what to ask you. This is a great opportunity for you to help them with clarifying questions.

"Peter, I sense your interest, but at the same time I sense there is something holding you back. Is there something still unresolved in your mind?

The "Scale of 1-to-10" Question
(With a brief summary to begin)

This is an another outstanding general question you can learn and use in a variety of situations to gauge your prospect's interest in your product or business offering.

A good way to start is by summing up or "prefacing."

"Jim, I really appreciate your interest and great questions. I'd really enjoy working with you and think we could build a successful business together..."

Scale of 1-10 Closing Question: *"I have an important question. (Then pause a moment) On a scale of 1-to-10, if 1 is low and 10 is high, how would you rate your interest in moving forward and getting started?*

Hint: If they say anything less than a 5, you're probably wasting your time. If they respond with 6-7, here's what to say:

"Great! What else would you need from me or need to know to move you to a 9 or 10?

If they respond with 8-10, here's what to say:

"Perfect, Jim. Let's get started. I'm excited about working with you. If you're like me you'll move to a 10 once you see what a great decision you've made"

Four Major Closing Mistakes

The first mistake is by far the biggest closing "crime" of them all.

1. Not Closing At All – One study showed that nearly 70% of sales presentations end without anyone asking the prospect to make a decision. Some people are so afraid of rejection or losing a sale that they never get around to a closing question. Don't waste all your preparation, your hard work or your valuable time by being afraid to ask closing questions. Refusal is not rejection. Prospects can never reject you. They can only reject what you are offering.

2. Closing Too Early – Sometimes it's not about *what* you ask, but *when* you ask. If you haven't truly connected and created rapport, qualified the prospect's needs and desires and offered a proper introduction of your product or opportunity, it may be too early to ask your prospect to commit. It's a lot like trying to withdraw money from the bank before you've made a deposit.

Be sure you've led your prospect through all the Power Prospecting steps; otherwise your closing question may be unproductive.

3. Closing Too Late – Don't wait too long. You can literally talk yourself out of helping a person decide by stretching out your presentation and putting off the important closing question. If you've gone through the steps, don't worry about seeming too aggressive. Remember, you're a professional; and people are silently begging to be led. Stop talking. Ask the CLOSING question!

4. Talking Past Closing Time – When you finally get to your closing question, ask it and then stop. Be absolutely silent. Remind yourself, *"If I'm the first person to talk after I ask my closing question then I lose."* Don't be afraid of the silence. Many sales are lost when you continue to talk past the magic moment. You may have just talked your prospect out of, if not *bored* your prospect out of the sale.

A Prospecting Mantra That Can Help You

This is a very useful tool and take away: Think of it as a mental warm-up and attitude check that will help you with your "closing mentality." Read it or say it to yourself often.

"I serve people by becoming a skilled closer. I serve people by helping them clarify what they want or need, or what they don't want or need."

"I serve people by helping them understand and crystallize what steps they should take to get what they want. I serve people by asking questions that help them save time and reduce stress. I accept the reality that no matter how skilled I am or how wonderful my products or opportunities are, some people are going to be interested and some are not!"

7. FOLLOW UP – To finish to completion; to follow through on; to increase the effectiveness or enhance the success of by further action.

Following up the right way is one of the most important yet underused high leverage activities in prospecting communications; it is simply one of the very best ways to serve people and demonstrate professionalism.

FOCUSED FOLLOW UP is what network-marketing professionals do. It means having a desired outcome for your "follow up conversation."

Research shows that almost 50% of sales people *never* follow up with a second contact; and another 25% make a second contact and stop.

Statistics also reveal that 80% of all sales are made on the fifth to twelfth contact. That means that the vast majority of the time sales are lost due to lack of follow up! In other words – there's a fortune to be made by learning to FOLLOW UP.

Following up is easy to do once you learn how – it's not difficult – but requires a little discipline and the right mindset.

There are three general objectives for following up:

1. Support the prospect in taking the next (agreed-upon) action step. (Examples could be; reviewing additional materials, trying your product, meeting your business partner, meeting their spouse, etc.)

2. To stay in touch with the prospect so you can be in a position to serve their needs if and when the opportunity arises.

3. Provide additional services or products after the sale of your product, service or opportunity; to strengthen and build the relationship.

Don't just follow up – follow up with a purpose – an objective. Clearly identify the reason for the communication and your intended outcome. Being focused means you have an outcome in mind and a specific reason for following up.

Good Reasons for Following Up

1. To remind someone of the time and directions for a meeting, introductory presentation or phone call.

2. To get a person's feedback and determine interest after they've reviewed a tool or sampled or experienced your product.

3. To reconnect and evaluate if the timing is better for them to try your product or review your business opportunity.

4. To determine if a person needs any additional information or has questions before they get started.

5. To demonstrate that the relationship is important to you; you care about their needs; to learn if you can continue to help them with your product or service.

The Rule of One

A technique that can help you improve your follow up communications is the Rule of One. Ask yourself these questions before any follow up:

"What is the single most important outcome I want to gain from this communication?

"What message do I want to send?

What is the ideal response?

What is the one thing I want to accomplish?"

Choose ONE outcome and write it down. Review it before you make your follow up call. Challenge yourself to have ONE intended outcome rather than several. The results can be remarkable.

Here are some examples.

Follow Up Questions
(With possible intended outcomes)

- Intended outcome: Set and agree on a meeting time

"Bill, last month you suggested I should get back with you at this time to see if your schedule had lightened up ...would now be a better time to (...meet my business partner ...attend my business mixer ...meet me for coffee?")

- Intended outcome: Set and agree on a meeting time

"Mary, you suggested I contact you once you got back from your vacation. Are you free for a few minutes this Tuesday night or would next Tuesday be better?"

- Intended outcome: Set and agree on a meeting time

"When we spoke last week you suggested I give you a call in a few days. Are you free on Thursday night?

- Intended outcome: Gain someone's feedback and opinion

"Dave, you had a look at our streaming video a few days ago. I really value your feedback and opinion. What did you like best?"

- Intended outcome: Gain someone's feedback and opinion

"Sue, I sent you the information you requested plus the link to our company website. Do you have a few minutes to share your initial impressions?"

- Intended outcome: Build the relationship and keep your promise

"Joanne, it's been several months since we spoke about my new business and I promised to give you a progress report. I really think you're going to enjoy hearing the news, so do you have a few minutes for a quick update?"

- Intended outcome: Build the relationship and keep your promise

"Hi Rick. You've been trying our product for over a month now. I'm really eager to get your impressions. What have you noticed? ...What do you like best?"

- Intended outcome: Build the relationship by being of service

"We just launched a new product (or service) and I thought you'd appreciate learning about what it's doing for people. Can I send you over some information or a link to a video overview?"

- Intended outcome: Build the relationship; stay in touch with their changing needs Intended outcome:

"The last time we spoke, you were reluctant to get involved because (...we just got started ...the timing was off for you ...you had just started a new job ...you were experiencing some challenges, etc.) Would you have a few minutes for a quick update?"

Make yourself indispensible. Stay aware of people's changing needs so you can be in a position to help them. Stay in touch. Foster and maintain the relationship.

Skillful follow up may help you make a comeback, even when you initially thought a person wasn't interested. Whether you're trying to recover someone's interest or keep a customer after the sale – practice *focused follow up*.

Some More Thoughts On The Power Prospecting Formula

For some people, learning and internalizing a "seven-step" model can seem difficult at first. I want to encourage you AND promise you that if you'll take the time to learn the model and add it to your skill set, it will pay huge, positive dividends.

In the next chapter, and especially in Chapters Four through Eleven that deal with some of the most common objections, you'll see the "model" running underneath all of the sample scripts.

With just a few hours of practice you will begin to get very comfortable and proficient. Once that happens, prospecting starts to get fun, *and* your effectiveness (and results) will grow impressively.

Finally, if you are more of a visual or auditory learner, or just want to reinforce what you've learned so far, please go to www.montetaylor.com/freestuff and subscribe so you can get immediate access to the free videos I've created on the Power Prospecting Formula. You can also get immediate access plus to other very useful reports and trainings.

Enjoy!

CHAPTER THREE

Managing Objections With AVVIS

Why Most Small Businesses Fail
(And what that has to do with managing objections)

Over 25 years ago, Michael E. Gerber wrote an outstanding book, *The E-Myth – Why Most Small Businesses Don't Work And What To Do About It*.

One of Gerber's key messages has stood the test of time: If you want to be successful in business, you must have a system (or model) to follow. Systems are duplicable and people are not.

If what you are doing is so complex or so stylized that others cannot see themselves doing it, then your business will grow slowly because it will rely totally on you.

What you want people to be thinking or saying is, " Yep, …I can do that."

In this chapter you'll learn the second system of "communication flow" which I call AVVIS. Again, I say system rather than technique; because a system means there is a plan to follow.

AVVIS and "We Try Harder"

Depending upon your age, you may or may not ever remember hearing the iconic Avis car rental company slogan: "*We're Number Two. We Try Harder*." Avis used the slogan as a branding statement for over 50 years. It was eventually shortened to, "*We Try Harder*" and passed into oblivion only recently.

The AVVIS system for handling objections has absolutely nothing to do with the car company. But, it is a salute to the idea of "trying just a little bit harder" or spending a little more time gathering information to manage a prospect's objection or concern.

It means learning a few more communication tools so you can help people gain even more clarity.

AVVIS is an acronym for Acknowledge/Verify/Validate/Isolate/Solve

Wait Just A Minute!

You might be asking yourself: Do I really need a second system if I've just learned the Listen/Feel/Felt/Found/Question system?

Me: *"Great question, Dear Reader. I hear you and I'm so glad you raised this issue."*

"You've just learned a simple system so why learn another one? I know exactly how you feel. I felt the same way; and so have others. I already have too much information in my head to remember all of it. I just want to start practicing one system before I learn another one!"

"But, Dear Reader, what I found was, after learning Feel, Felt, Found, AVVIS was SO easy to learn. And, it gave me even more tools to handle any objection. Honestly, it was like falling off a log."

"So, Dear Reader, if taking just a few more minutes would take your skills to the stratosphere, are you open to continuing?"

Got the point?

The AVVIS System

AVVIS is actually similar to Listen/Feel/Felt/Found/Question.

However, AVVIS has two slight variations: The "I" in AVVIS reminds us to "Isolate" the objection, plus place more emphasis on making sure you are solving the problem; which is the "**S**" in AVVIS

Remember, the problem is expressed as the objection (fear, concern, question, belief, etc.)

Note: The AVVIS system will work much better if you begin with *careful listening* and always end with a *question*, just as in system one.

AVVIS is: Acknowledge/Verify/Validate/Isolate/Solve with **Listen** at the front and **Question** on the end.

This is easy. You already know **Listen** (to the Objection) and **Question** (after expressing Feel/Felt/Found) where you ask questions to make sure they are ready to move forward and take the next steps.

And you already know Acknowledge/Verify/Validate, which is very similar to Feel/Felt/Found

Remember?

"Mary I know how you feel. I'm so glad you brought this up. A lot of people feel the same way...they're just not comfortable with what feels like selling at first."

You've already seen an example of Validate:

Prospect: *"So, is this one of those pyramids?"* Or *"...is this network marketing?"*

You: *"Mary, good question. If you don't mind, tell me, …what's your experience with network marketing?"*

Note: You just used a clarifying (or Validating) question to help you validate that this is a real concern.

After all, they might say, after you've asked the "Validating" question.

Prospect: *"Great! We have lots of experience in network marketing and have been looking for a good company."*

Surprise! You we're about to spend several wasted minutes defending your industry.

So what's the main difference in the two systems?

The difference is to further develop and heighten your ability to clarify by first isolating the objection.

Isolating means you are separating the objection, partly to learn if this is the real objection or simply something they've thrown out, but is not necessarily the prime objection. Prime objections are the "deal stoppers" if not managed correctly.

The "S" for Solve helps you remember to ask questions to make sure you've addressed (solved) the concern or objection, and if you can, get the prospect to acknowledge that you've solved the concern.

It may be that they agree to participate in addressing their own concern by reading, listening or watching something that can educate them and therefore "solve" their concern.

AVVIS requires just a little more practice and skill, but if you can learn to ride a bicycle, (Feel/Felt/Found) then you can learn to ride a bicycle on a rocky trail or at high speed (AVVIS) with a bit more practice.

Skilled communicators will learn and use both.

AVVIS IN ACTION

Prospect: *"I just don't think I could sell. I'm very uncomfortable selling."*

You: *"Mary, I'm so glad you brought this up. A lot of people feel the same way. Tell me about some of your experiences with selling."*

Then the prospect shares their experiences; which are mostly negative. What you learn as she tells her story is that she worked for a company that didn't give her any training and expected her to sink or swim. She hated the feeling that she didn't know what she was doing or what to say.

You also learn that she's on the PTA and loves working with the teachers and other parents to gain consensus for projects and fundraisers, and is passionate about contributing and "helping people."

You: *"Mary, thanks so much for telling me about yourself and sharing what you love, and also what concerns you. Other than what you feel about "the selling aspect" of our business, do you have any other concerns?*

That, by the way is *isolating* the concern, which is the "I" in AVVIS!

Prospect: *"Not really. Well, maybe just about how much time I'd have to have to dedicate to this to be successful."*

You: *"I'm so glad you brought up the subject of time; it's an important point. I'm curious; if you had to guess at how much time you might have each week to dedicate to a worthy project, what would you say?"*

Again you're *listening, acknowledging, validating,* and *isolating* the time concern.

Mary answers, "About 10-12 hours a week. That's all I have."

Bingo! Now you SOLVE.

You: *"Mary, on your first point about sales. Here's my question; if you knew for sure that we could train anyone who's willing and coachable so they were comfortable and effective in just a short time, would that help? Would you be willing to come to our "Learn To Sell Without Really Selling" seminar next weekend so you can see first hand how well our trainings work for people like you and me?"*

Prospect: *"Sure."*

You: *"That's perfect! Honestly I'm thrilled! And, to address your point about time, which I'm glad you brought up, I'm happy to report there is no problem. If you can truly dedicate 10-12 hours a week and do the things we teach you to do, you can be successful."*

"Mary, almost everyone in our business works part-time so we have created systems and trainings that honor and respect your time. Most people, including me, started very part-time and we are building great businesses with just a few dedicated hours a week."

Now, Question (Close).

"Mary, I enjoy your energy, enthusiasm and your questions. I really feel we could be successful together. Would you like to know what the next steps are and how to get started?"

If Mary brings up another concern at this point, what do you do?

Easy. Repeat either system.

Listen/Feel/Felt/Found/Question OR

Listen/AVVIS/Question

Remember, *Listen* is the always the first step of BOTH of the systems and *Question* is always the last step.

Some Final Thoughts

Either of these systems will work for you. Practicing and learning them will reap great rewards. If you stay focused on "being their helper" or "thinking partner" you will be surprised at how easy it will be to handle any objection.

We are rewarded in life for the questions we help answer. We are rewarded in life for being able to help people verbalize their problems, and if possible, solve them.

We are rewarded in life for understanding what others need and helping them meet their needs if we can. We are rewarded in life by helping people achieve clarity. Without clarity it's almost impossible to move forward and succeed.

Stand For People's Success

When you are addressing people's concerns, objections, questions or problems, the feeling you want them to have is that you "stand for their success" by helping them learn and work through their issues.

Help people clarify what they want (or don't want). Help people make better decisions and help people crystallize the steps they need to take to get what they say they want.

If you can learn to stand for other's success by providing clarity, you can become a master prospector and a master communicator.

When The Outcome Is "No"

Your goal is to improve communications with people in a way that helps them achieve positive outcomes. A positive outcome COULD be helping them decide NOT to purchase your product or service because for some reason it's not right for them.

In some circles the end game is to make the sale or close the deal at almost any cost. For a variety of reasons this doesn't work well in network marketing – certainly not for the long term.

Pushing people into an unhealthy "buying decision" or a poor "joining decision" doesn't help people. It doesn't help you or them. Network marketing is a "relationship industry."

Push people who don't really want to buy your product or to join your organization and they'll be gone in a matter of weeks, if not days.

Sometimes NO is OK!

In the next chapters we'll share more sample conversations on specific objections and offer more examples of QUESTION/ FEEL/FELT/FOUND/QUESTION and AVVIS, in action.

Once you've completed chapters four through eleven, you will have been exposed to perhaps 90% of the most common objections.

Soon you will be able to handle any prospect's question, concern, or objection with ease.

CHAPTER FOUR

What If Someone Asks, "Is This One Of Those Pyramid Things?"

The Pyramid Scheme Objection

Another variation of this is, "Is this MLM or Network Marketing?"

My best guess is this is one of the more frequent "push backs" you'll come across when speaking to prospects, and certainly a question most network marketers want to learn how to handle comfortably.

A year or so ago I was interviewing one of the very top network marketers in the industry. In addition to building a massive organization he has a solid reputation as an educator, trainer and best-selling author.

In the interview I asked him how he handled this objection. He said, "Honestly, it doesn't come up for me that often because my belief is so strong. It's unshakeable. The industry is not on trial – it's simply one of the most positive, people-empowering business endeavors I've ever experienced."

"Work on **your personal belief** first," he said. People, who don't believe completely and wholeheartedly in the industry seem for some unknown reason to attract more prospects that question the validity of it.

Before we suggest some scripts and concepts to better handle this objection, let me strongly suggest that you honestly evaluate your own beliefs about the industry you've chosen.

Plug in, for a moment, to your personal beliefs. If you are anything less than a solid nine on a scale of one to ten, I highly recommend you read Robert T. Kiyosaki's book, *The Business of the 21st Century*.

Kiyosaki is also the author of the New York Times best seller, *Rich Dad, Poor Dad,* and many other books. If you haven't already, add it to your library and read it. Google the title and you'll quickly see several places where you can order it.

Another similar resource, available as a DVD, is *Brilliant Compensation*, by Tim Sales, which you can find online by searching First Class MLM Tools.

So what's going on in the minds of people who seem to object to or have concerns about the network marketing industry? Here are some possibilities.

(1) They may have been involved in some fashion in the past or know someone who had a less than positive experience.

(2) They have no personal experience whatsoever other than they've heard something negative somewhere (can't remember what it was or who said it) and they more or less toss it out as a delaying tactic or "automatic script" when the subject comes up.

(3) They have a friend or family member that "hounded" them to get involved and would rather not be in a business where you have to "beg or badger" people to buy or join.

(4) Sometimes the prospect simply has doubts, expressed or unexpressed, that they have what it takes to succeed at network marketing, so instead they condemn the industry.

AVVIS Takes On That "Pyramid Thing"

Before we begin, here are several important "mindful prospecting" tips that will help you prepare to manage this objection, question or concern:

1. Always start by building rapport (remember CONNECT?) with the person by taking a sincere posture of, "I'm very interested in learning more about your perspective."

This is the perfect time for you to remember to bring your, "...seek first to understand, then be understood" attitude to the conversation. It's a "highly effective habit!

2. Relax. Be patient. There is simply no dazzling, super "one-size-fits all" response to overcome this objection. Snappy "one liners" and desperation never work.

Some of the most talented and successful professional network marketers took weeks or months evaluating the industry before they committed themselves.

There are hundreds "how I got started stories" where professional networkers admit that regardless of any initial objections they had, the "game changer" was "timing ...and their readiness for change." In other words, the timing was right in their life and they were ready to make some changes.

3. Make SURE you have established the person's need: perhaps more time freedom; more money; security; desire to work from home; whatever. Then CONNECT the need to their agreement to learn or discover the real benefits of the network marketing industry opportunity.

Of course, one of the very best tools for managing this objection is AVVIS:

Listen/**Acknowledge/Verify/Validate/Isolate/Solve**/Question

Prospect: *"Is this one of those pyramid schemes?"* Or: *"Is this network marketing?"*

Acknowledge

"Is that a concern, Bill? What's your experience with network marketing?" Or,

"John, are you worried that this is one of those pyramid schemes?" Or,

"Mary, are you concerned that this is one of those pyramid schemes you've heard of in the news?"

Validate

"I'm glad you brought that up. Sometimes there are articles in the news about pyramid schemes, but this isn't one of them; this is a legitimate, reputable company."

"Thanks for mentioning this, Sue. Some people make the mistake of comparing network marketing to a pyramid scheme. The difference is, pyramid schemes are illegal and this is a legitimate business."

Isolate

"Is that your main concern when you think about having your own home-based business, or is their anything else?"

"Other than your question about being a pyramid scheme, which it's not, is there anything else that you're concerned about?"

Solve (and Question)

"Would you be willing to invest some time reading and learning about our industry from a New York Times best selling author? … and give me your follow-up impressions afterwards?"

"I'm sure you've heard of the billionaire investor, Warren

Buffet, yes? Donald Trump, yes? Did you know that Buffet's fund has invested in several top network marketing companies and Trump has featured and recommended the industry on his show?"

"Would you be willing to invest a little time learning about our industry from our company DVD called (FILL IN THE BLANK)?...And then give me your follow up impressions?"

"Would you be O.K. with setting the business aside for a moment and making a commitment to experience our product. We can talk about business later, O.K?"

Objections are usually a request – sometimes an awkward request – for more information or a way to avoid or delay making a decision. The key is to *avoid a debate* and try not to focus on convincing the person.

However, if your company has a tool such as a DVD, fact sheet or CD, with some impressive data and credibility, now is the time to bring it up and present it to the prospect.

Once you accept that objections are normal, natural and even positive, and usually just a request for more information, a lot of your fear will vanish.

Avoid being defensive. Remember, what your prospect is more than likely afraid of is the risk involved. Most reputable companies offer a money back guarantee on products or distributor packages, so make sure your prospect is aware of any guarantees.

Think about your own experiences when you joined a network marketing company. What were your concerns; your main objections? It's more than likely that some of your prospects will have the same ones too.

As you hear about some of the greatest success stories in network marketing, you will realize that no one comes into this business without questions and objections. Many very successful people first said "NO!" And some of the very top leaders in network marketing initially said "NO" several times!

Realize in your "prospecting communications," that the person you're speaking with, on some level, is looking at you as the potential coach, mentor and leader. In a way you are always "auditioning" when you are handling their objections.

Master prospectors plan to have a very good audition – even if they don't get the part.

Just accept the fact and have some fun with it.

CHAPTER FIVE

What If Someone Says, "I Don't Have Any Time"?

Time Is A Choice

The key to what to say when someone says, "I don't have any time," is to make sure that you understand what they're really saying before you structure your response. One of the best ways to do this is to first ask an "expanding question."

In fact, get in to the habit of asking expanding questions automatically when you hear almost any objection. This is what expert communicators do. Here's an example.

You: *"June, I hear what you're saying and I understand. Tell me more about your time constraints. What's going on with you currently?"*

Then the prospect describes how busy they are. Listen carefully. Just remember that everyone is busy, or feels busy; and we all have the same 24 hours a day. No more, no less.

You: FEEL, FELT, FOUND, QUESTION

"June, I know how you feel about being so busy. In the beginning I couldn't imagine where I could find the time to start a new business. I also knew that if I didn't carve out a just a few hours a week, I'd still be worrying and feeling frustrated about having no time next year and the year after that. What I found was that with what my business partner showed me and what the company offers, I'm actually using a very small amount of time to build a successful business."

Now your QUESTION:

*"June, if I could show you how to get your time back
…honestly, if I could show you how to build this business and
make money while you're sleeping or doing something else,
would you be open to learning more?"*

What? Make money while you're sleeping? Are you kidding?

No. Today, almost all network marketing companies have
"presentation tools" such as streaming videos and audio,
downloadable DVD's, CD's and mobile apps with compelling
presentations, product overviews, follow-up tools and training.

Some companies offer automated marketing; follow-up "drip
email campaigns" and websites that do some of the
presentation "heavy lifting."

It's become an automated, and more importantly, an
asynchronous world; which means multiple activities can be
going on at different times in different time zones! Prospects
can be viewing or listening to your presentation; customers
can be ordering your product; distributors can be trained, and
you can be making money while you're sleeping or doing
something else.

Here are some other possible responses.

(This one is fairly aggressive but works well if you are
confident and know you can help them.)

*"June, thanks for bringing up the time issue. The truth is I
really don't need your time. Are you open to learning what I
mean by that?"*

I've used this response successfully with busy professionals,
health care professionals, lawyers and time-strapped
executives. I explain what I really need is people in their circle
of influence and really just a few of those. Within their circle of
influence are people who have business experience,

…leadership qualities, … people strongly motivated by money… who may be open to an attractive business venture.

I may also add…

"It may be someone who …feels he/she is not being paid what he/she is worth …or is not spending enough free time with his/her family …or perhaps someone who is not completely happy with the kind of work they are doing."

I go on to explain that if they can refer qualified people to me, I'll handle the presentation; using tools, plus handle the follow-up. Of course, all their contacts will be sponsored in "their business" which will benefit both of us.

I'll add at the end…

"Jim, we'll be building your business with my time and your contacts. After we get some real traction and success we can discuss taking your business to the next level." Meaning we can reevaluate their time priorities later.

Some other responses:

"I've found that people will never have more time unless they find a way to make more money. Would you even be open to me helping you solve your time issue? Is that something that's important to you?"

"Bill, if time is tough now, how do you envision your future from a time standpoint if you don't try to do something – by something, I mean create a plan now?"

Remember: Always use LISTEN, FEEL, FELT, FOUND, QUESTION or AVVIS as your system.

Over the years people have asked, "How do you always seem to know what to say?"

The answer is a system: LISTEN, FEEL, FELT, FOUND, QUESTION or AVVIS, and a sincere desire to help people find clarity in their lives. I've learned to use that clarity to help people achieve financial or physical peace of mind – and so can you!

Of course, some people may simply stonewall you with an unexpressed objection. When they say they "have no time" it's the first thing they could think of to change or end the conversation. They're simply not interested.

If you sense a truly negative energy from the conversation, just thank them and move on. There are many thousand's, if not millions, of people waiting and open to what you have to offer.

If you want to leave the door open you can say something like this…

"Dave, I sense with your current schedule this really is a bad time for you. When would be a better time?"

If they give you a firm time and date, put it on your calendar and follow up at the agreed time.

You can also use the, "Who Do You Know …That You Could Recommend To Me" referral technique which you'll learn in the next chapter, Chapter Six – "Selling" Objections.

More "No Time" Objections

What to say when people say they don't have any time or are too busy:

"I'm really glad you brought up how busy you are. Many of my team members said the same thing in the beginning. You might be surprised to learn that many of the top networkers earning full-time incomes are only working 10-20 hours a

week. That's because they've built a business that leverages other people's time."

"Bill, if I can show you how, in just a few hours a week, with effort, over the next 12 to 24 months you could potentially match or even double your current income, what would you say?"

By the way, this is an opportunity to use a "time leverage napkin presentation." Money projections are inappropriate but time leverage projections are appropriate and real eye-openers.

You can do this on a napkin or a piece of paper. If the person is on the phone, have them take out a piece of paper and follow along as you explain.

Time Leverage Napkin Presentation

Start by writing the number 2 on a napkin or a piece of paper and then double the two every month for a total of 12 months, just like the illustration below.

Say this while you're adding the numbers:

"Month 1 you enroll 2 people, who spend 20 hours average each month on their business. That's just 5 hours a week (less than 1 hour a day). Month 2 every new person enrolls two each who average 20 hours each month on their business. Month 3, the same thing ...all the way to 12 months."

Month 1 = 2 people
Month 2 = 4 people (2x2)
Month 3 = 8 people (2x4)
Month 4 = 16 people (2x8)
Month 5 = 32 people (2x16)
Month 6 = 64 people (2x32)
Month 7 = 128 people (2x64)
Month 8 = 256 people (2x128)

Month 9 = 512 people (2x256)
Month 10 = 1024 people (2x512)
Month 11 = 2048 people (2x1024)
Month 12 = 4096 people (2x2048)

"Now, when you get to month 12, you'll have 4,096 people in your business spending 20 hours a month. At the end of one year, that would be over 81,000 hours (4096 X 20 = 81,920) each month working for you in your business."

Of course, some people will spend more than 20 hours a week and others less. This is a reasonable projection based on most people working part-time; 5 hours a week.

"If the average workweek for employees is 40 hours, then 81,920 hours is like having 512 employees in your business who you don't have to supervise or pay."

As the clincher, ask them, *"How many did you enroll?"*

Answer: *"Just the first two."*

Now that's time leverage!

Here's another response to, "I have no time." (Sometimes people just need some leadership, some clarity and a gentle nudge.)

"Dave, I'm really glad that you said you're too busy, because I'm really busy too. Here's what I've learned; people that are busy get things done in a fraction of the time the "I'm not busy" people seem to need. Busy people are productive. I'm looking for busy people."

"If you can carve out just a few focused hours each week we can achieve amazing results together. We'll start by leveraging my time and my knowledge and a few of your contacts. One of my visions for the future is that neither of us ever says we're too busy again unless we say, "We're just too

busy having fun and making money."

"What do you say?"

"Shall we get started?"

Here's a shorter version. Use only after you listen and acknowledge their time issue.

"Bill, if you knew for sure that we could take just a few hours each week by focusing on high leverage activities to get you the results you want …that we could work together building this business part time until you achieve the income levels you want …what would you say?"

I have found that the best way to give advice is find out what people want then advise them to do it.

HARRY S. TRUMAN

CHAPTER SIX

What If Someone Says, "I Don't Like To Sell"?

"Selling" Objections

Before we learn how to manage this objection, let's visit the perception of sales, sales people and the definition of "selling." Most of us have heard someone say something negative about selling or salespeople.

Maybe you've said it yourself.

"I can't sell."
"I don't like to sell."
"I don't want to have to talk people into buying anything."
"I don't like most sales people."
"I don't want to be pushy."
"I could never do that.

Many people believe learning to handle objections is what sales people do. Some form of, "I can't sell." Or, "I don't want to sell." is perhaps one of the top five objections you can expect to hear from prospects.

Once again, you are going to have to first recognize, examine and deal with your own beliefs, because your personal beliefs definitely enter into the prospecting equation.

Simply An Exchange Of Values

The late master teacher, Leyland Val Van De Wall offered this definition of selling. He called it a simple truth.

"Selling is nothing more than an exchange of values."

To clarify, he added, *"Exchanging values requires only a way to communicate and a desire to help each other get what you want. If you focus on helping people get what they want, you can create the environment to also get what you want."*

Some people don't recognize a good salesperson when they come across one because the exchange was so enjoyable and painless. When the exchange is well handled it doesn't feel like a sale; It feels like's two people simply enjoying a happy and mutually beneficial exchange of values.

Most people like to buy, but don't want to be sold. On the other hand, people admire, respect and buy from others who learn what they want (value) and are willing to help them get what they want.

Keep your intention on helping people. Your goal is to ethically help resolve people's buying concerns and issues. Part of the value you offer is providing clarity by listening and asking good questions so you can help them make a decision to buy, purchase, engage or get involved; if that serves their best interests.

Here are more ideas of what to say when people say, "I can't sell." or "I don't like to sell."

"Larry, I'm really glad you brought this up. You might be surprised to know that I don't like being sold …and a lot of people feel the same way."

"What has really made the difference is that I quit trying to be in sales and instead learned how to be in the "invitation business." Honestly, what I do every day is invite people to watch a streaming video, invite people to listen to a CD, invite people to watch a business tour online, invite people to read something interesting. I don't sell people; I just invite them because it's much more enjoyable."

"Here's my question, Larry. If I can show you a completely different way to sell; if I can show you how to make money by simply inviting people to take a look at something that has the potential to change their lives in a positive way, would you be open to getting started?"

Or, Joanne says, *"I just don't want to sell."*

"That's great, because we focus on recommending and referring. Have you ever mentioned a great restaurant or recommended a movie to a friend? Did you ever get paid for the recommendation? Our business will pay you for recommending something that you already believe in."

Or,

"Perfect! Neither do we! Instead, we show people how to hand out tools that do the talking for them with a professionally crafted presentation. We are the messengers, not the message."

The "Two Definitions of Selling" Response

"Bill, thanks, I'm glad you shared your feelings about selling. You are way too intelligent for us to split hairs on the subject of selling. Are you open to hearing another perspective?"

If they nod or say, "Yes," then continue.

"Would you agree, Bill, that one definition of selling is trying to get people to buy something they neither need nor want? Do you agree with that definition?"

"Would you agree that another possible definition of selling is simply sharing your love or passion for a product or service with people who are going to welcome hearing about it ...and will thank you for sharing what's in your heart?"

"What if you knew that there are millions of people waiting to hear about what we have? If you knew that for sure, what would you say?"

"If you knew my team was using our tools to find people who thank us, congratulate us and even hug us for sharing what we have, what would you say?"

"If I could show you how together we can find the people that are looking for what we have, would you be ready for the next steps?"

Of course, remember the old adage; *"A person convinced against their will is of the same opinion still."* Some people have cherished personal beliefs, attitudes and fears about money, selling and business that will never change.

The most important belief you can have is your personal belief about what you're offering. Never try to convince. Simply make sure you clearly understand your prospect's view. Offer them another possible perspective and if nothing changes, move on; but first ask them whom they know!

Who Do You Know That You Could Recommend to Me?

If you find a person is very resistant or simply not interested, always take the opportunity to ask for a third party referral, or what I like to call a, "Who Do You Know?" recommendation.

It goes like this:

First thank them for spending the time with you (or listening to you, or considering your opportunity/product).

"Bill, it seems like this is not the right timing for you… but thanks for taking a look. Could I ask you for a small favor?"

If they say, "Yes" or "What is it?" …Go ahead and ask.

"Who do you know, that you could recommend to me, that has either some business experience, some leadership qualities or is strongly motivated by money… and may be open to an attractive business venture?"

"Who do you know who feels he/she is not being paid what he/she is worth …or is not spending enough free time with his/her family …or perhaps someone who is not completely happy with the kind of work they are doing?"

Important note: Don't ask them to "recommend YOU to someone." Ask them to "recommend someone TO you" who fits the criteria you mentioned in your question.

If they can't think of anyone, thank them again for considering and close the conversation:

"Fair enough. Thanks! If you do happen to think of someone in the future who fits my description, please let me know."

If they do give you a name, thank them and say this:

"Thank you! Is there anyone else that comes to mind?"

(You may want to repeat your criteria to jog their memory.)

Once you have the name or names, close the conversation and thank them again.

"Bill, I really appreciate the name (or names) you gave me; and if it's all right with you, may I get back to you or send you a note with a brief report on their response?"

Most people will say yes. This leaves the door open for you to re-contact them.

Imagine if the person they recommended to you has a positive response or gets happily involved with your product, service or business venture?

Be sure to contact the "referring person" and let them know the good news. Who knows? They may reconsider after learning that the person they recommended saw something they may have missed seeing the first time around.

By the way, if you have an outstanding product, service or opportunity, there are millions of people open to learning about how you can help make their lives better.

CHAPTER SEVEN

What If Someone Says, "I Don't Have Any Money"?

Wealth Is Knowing What You Want

Before you share your business with prospects it is important to find a way to uncover whether or not they have a real need for the business, or your products, before you actually do a presentation or concerning yourself with managing objections.

Whenever possible, make sure that you understand their wants, needs and desires so you can structure your response. Again, and I'll say this over and over, one of the best ways to do this is to get in to the habit of first asking "expanding questions."

For example, say... *"May I ask you a question?"* (Pause and wait for their response.)

"What's important to you right now?"

"What is it that you want out of life that you don't have right now?"

"What is it you complain to yourself about the most? ...Not about yourself... but to yourself?"

"What is it that you'd like to have, or what would you do if money were no object?"

"What's going on in your life right now that you'd love to have a solution for?"

It's important to understand that most people want the same things; more money, time, freedom, vibrant health, meaningful relationships and a feeling that they're getting ahead in life or perhaps making a positive difference for others.

Most people, however they describe it or express it, are looking for financial, physical and mental peace of mind.

Become good at painting a "solutions picture" for your prospect. This is not so much about the product you are selling – it's more about how what you're offering can help them reach their dreams. Let them see that what you have is an opportunity for them to achieve peace of mind.

If you are good at asking questions and painting vivid pictures that address their needs, you will be able to avoid having the money objection come up, or when it does, you will be able to handle it with ease.

Always keep AVVIS in the back of your mind: (ACKNOWLEDGE, VALIDATE/VERIFY, ISOLATE, SOLVE) Consider responding first with an expanding question. If they say, *"I don't have the money,"* here are a few responses, or expanding questions, that may work for you:

"I know how you feel and perhaps what you're going through. I also know you know it takes a little bit of investment to start any business. How were you imagining you'd start this business?"

"Wow, how does that feel?" Pause and wait for an answer then ask, *"Are you going to let that stop you from getting the things in your life that you say you want?"*

"Is it really that you don't have the money, or are you just saying that so that you don't hurt my feelings?"

"I can appreciate that you don't have the money, but if you did have the money, would you be ready to join us right now?"

"I hear you. Let me just ask you, if money were not an issue, what would you do with your time? Would you travel, buy a new house, car, or visit the best cities in the world? What would you do?"

"Say a black Mercedes was parked out front and the only thing keeping you from owning it was $500 and 60 days working part-time. What would you say?"

Help your prospect get clarity. Help them paint a picture of what life would be like for them if money were no object. Help them see the steps they need to take to get what it is they say they want. Help them see whatever it is that's getting in the way – what's stopping them from getting what they want.

Don't be "preachy." It annoys most people. A good way to keep from sounding preachy is to use the system: LISTEN (AVVIS) and ask QUESTIONS.

Don't forget to SOLVE!

"Deb, if I could show you how to get your business started, plus get the small investment you made back in less than 30 days, with a profit, what would you say?"

Help them see that the money is not an expense, but an investment in their dreams for the future.

"Wealth is <u>knowing</u> what you want. Unhappiness is <u>not knowing</u> what you really want and killing yourself to get it."

If you want a place in the sun, you must leave the shade of the family tree.

OSAGE SAYING

CHAPTER EIGHT

What If Someone Says, "I Want To Think About It"?

Getting Things Out On The Table

No matter what type of product, service or opportunity you are offering, at some point you will hear the forward progress stopping, and the, "I want to think about it." response.

The "I want to think about it," or "Let me think about it," objection causes many network marketers to stumble on their words. Power prospectors seldom stumble; so let's make sure that this doesn't happen to you.

The "Let me think about it," objection is usually an unexpressed objection and the perfect opportunity for you to ask an "expanding question."

Don't forget; unexpressed objections are vague and perhaps reflect some concern or question that the person hasn't yet shared. On the other hand, it just may be that it's not a good time to introduce anything new into their life.

Your objective is to see if you can get the question, concern or objection on the table.

AVVIS is your system for handling, "I want to think about it."

First LISTEN then VALIDATE:

"Of course, no problem. I've always felt it's important to give some thought before making important decisions."

(Then ask your expanding and clarifying QUESTION):

"Before you go, may I ask you something?" Get their agreement before continuing.

"Usually when I say I have to think about something it means one of three things; either I have a problem with the price, a problem with the product or there's something not yet clear to me. Which one of these is it for you?"

Most times the prospect will appreciate your openness because you respectfully allowed them to be frank with you and perhaps get the real reason off their chest. Give them an opportunity to express their real objection.

Be careful asking people what they think. They may say, *"I'll have to think about it."*

It's always better to ask people what they *liked best about what they saw or heard*, rather than what they *thought* about it.

"How did you feel about the information you saw?"

"Tell me, what really caught your attention?"

Here's a simple "general question" you can use any time after a presentation or after someone says, *"I have to think about it."* It can help you understand what a person is thinking/feeling and to tactfully redirect them into a slightly different conversation for clarity and possible next steps:

"Mary, I'm pleased you want to think about it. May I ask you something?"

(Pause for their response.)

"After everything you've seen so far; do you see yourself as more of a product person, a business builder, or both?"

If their continuing response is still something like, *"I still have to think about it,"* you can try this:

"Mary, I'm actually a "think about it" person too. When I say, "I need to think about it," there's usually some research I need to do, something I need to read or see or know. While you're thinking about it, would you also be willing to …(watch this DVD, listen to this CD, watch this streaming video, read this booklet, etc.?)

If you are clear on the person's need (extra income, time freedom, dissatisfaction with their current job or career, etc.) then you may want to reconnect them with their "pain" and summarize:

"Brad, I understand you want to think about things …it's important. I know your issue of wanting to find a way to have more time with your family is also important to you, and I'm looking forward to working together to achieve your goal. When would you like for us to get back together?"

Remember, what you are doing is "leading the communications" and helping people take the appropriate next steps. You're helping people clarify their thoughts and make decisions. You are not trying to convince a person; something that doesn't work and doesn't serve anyone's interests in the long term.

You are "driving for clarity" for you and for the prospect.

If you want clarity, learn to take the lead and ask better QUESTIONS!

Gardens are not made by singing "Oh, how beautiful," and then sitting in the shade.

RUDYARD KIPLING

CHAPTER NINE

What If Someone Says, "I Need To Talk To My Spouse"?

While this objection doesn't appear as often as some others, managing this or other objections can be stressful if you are not prepared.

It might surprise you to learn that 8-10 or so of the objections your prospects offer will likely represent 98% of all the objections you'll EVER hear.

But don't forget, a Power Prospector's job is to listen without prejudging (Don't interrupt, pay attention) and of course your secret weapon is AVVIS.

- ACKNOWLEDGE the objection (*I hear you.*)
- VERIFY (*"Did you mean _____?"* or, *"Is this what you mean?"*)
- VALIDATE and identify with it (*I know how you feel, I felt that way too.*)
- ISOLATE the objection (*"Is this your most important/only concern? What else?"*)
- SOLVE the problem (*"If I could show you a way… If there was a way…"*)

Question (Confirm the solution and next steps)

By following the flow of AVVIS, you'll be able to overcome most network marketing objections.

The "I need to talk to my spouse," objection is one of the top ten network marketing objections in my experience. It is a little trickier than some because the last thing you want to do is alienate someone's spouse or make them feel uncomfortable with the idea that they want to seek support or permission from their spouse.

The first thing you want to know; is this objection true? Are they really looking to get input from their spouse or is it a way for them to avoid or delay making a decision. Here's a response that can help. It subtly covers all the bases (AVVIS) in one question:

"Sue, I understand, and I would never ask you to make a decision without your husband's (or significant other's) feedback. Open communication is what makes relationships work…"

Now here's your clarifying question:

"…If you ask your husband, and he agrees that whatever you want to do with the business is O.K and he supports you, would you be ready to get started today?"

If they waffle, or say anything but "Yes," then you haven't isolated their *real* objection and have more questions to ask to get to the real problem.

Here's something else you can try. If nothing else, it may help YOU get clarity:

"Sue, would you be open with me if I ask you a sincere question? Do you really need your husband's approval or are you just saying it so you don't hurt my feelings?"

It's a fair question, and one you can use for a variety of objections when you're not sure a person is being completely open with you.

Be careful not to say, *"Be honest with me,"* or *"Tell me the truth."* To some people, by just using these words you are implying dishonesty. Instead invite them to be "sincere" or "open."

Here's one more:

"Jane, I sense your excitement and you seem ready to join us except for wanting your husband's "buy-in." Would that be fair to say?"

If they say "yes." Then continue.

"To be fair to your spouse and you, when would you suggest we show the business presentation to your husband, in a way that can get him excited and on board?"

You've put it on the table. If they're truly ready to get started and don't have any more "stuff," then you've confirmed their desire to get started and now you are asking them how best to proceed so they can get what they want.

It is crucial to understand that if the timing is wrong for people, or people aren't ready for a change in their life, no matter how effective you are at approaching people and overcoming their objections, they will not be open to what you have to offer.

There is no security in this life.
There is only opportunity

DOUGLAS MACARTHUR

CHAPTER TEN

What If Someone Asks, "Can You Promise Me I'll Make Money?"

"Promises, Promises"

This question doesn't come up that often, but when it does, you'll want to be prepared.

Usually what the person is looking for is some assurance. Most people, assuming they have a real need for the business opportunity you're offering, are looking for the answers to four questions before they make a decision to move forward:

1. Do I like you?
2. Do I trust you?
3. Will you help me?
4. Do you have a plan for me to follow and get started?

Sometimes people will ask you this way:

"Can you promise me a big income? Can you promise me I'll make thousands of dollars?"

Here is an appropriate response to this question. It puts the focus squarely back on the individual's efforts, where it belongs.

"Mike, the simple truth is no one can promise you that because no one but you knows how much effort, energy and passion you'll bring to the table."

"There are two things that I can promise you:

"One is, if you don't do anything …nothing will change."

"Two is, if you do decide to move forward with us, if you stay focused, stay coachable and keep working consistently we'll make money together and we'll have fun together. You'll be working with a team of people invested in your success. You'll have the opportunity to join the tens of thousands of professional network marketers that are earning full-time incomes with part-time effort."

"Mike, what do you say?"

Always share the details of how you will work with them and support their efforts to achieve their goals. Make sure you are clear on the duplicable system the company or your up line leadership uses to launch and support new team members.

CHAPTER ELEVEN

How Can You Make Your Communications Sizzle?

There's a saying that you don't get a second chance to make a first impression.

Nowhere is this truer than in personal selling or prospecting communications. Whether you're making a phone call, speaking with a small group or one-on-one to an individual, you have just a few seconds, if that, to make people want to hear or learn more.

Big businesses spend millions creating a brand image or identity for their products. In network marketing, you are your own brand identity.

YOU must create your own positive marketing message.

Here are several ways to help you create the strong positive image you want to portray and position yourself as a credible professional.

Your Twenty-Second Sizzle Introduction

Learn to introduce yourself with a "twenty-second sizzle" intro. Have you ever been introduced to someone and after a minute or two you're at a complete loss for words because you still have no idea what it is they do or how to extricate yourself from the conversation? Overly technical jargon or wordy descriptions sap everyone's energy and help conversations end quickly.

Make sure that after meeting you and hearing about your company, people don't walk away thinking, "So what?" or "Huh?" More often than not, the response is muddled (if not evasive) and does little to create interest or curiosity in the person who asked you the question.

Be memorable. Create an interesting twenty-five word "sizzling sound bite" that tells who you are, what market you serve and provokes interest. Be sure a 7th grader could understand your message.

Confusing: *"I'm the CEO of TruthTech. We use the latest video transcription software algorithms to program computers for trial experts and their stakeholders to support high profile legal cases with elevated risk exposure and blah, blah, blah"*

Much Better: *"Hi, I'm Bill Williams. My company is TruthTech. We specialize in software to help determine if a trial witness is being truthful or not."*

Sell what people are interested in. People who are new to prospecting (and selling) often miss this point; people are only interested in solving their own problems. Make sure when you're speaking or presenting that you are showing people how to solve their problems with your product, service or opportunity.

"I work with people who are tired of dieting. My name is Jill Friendly and I have a proven, no diet – no exercise weight loss program called the Friendly Plan."

Be ready! Your "sizzling sound bite" can also be your response to the question, "What do you do for a living? Always respond by focusing on the value you give to the person you're speaking with.

"My name is Susanne James and I specialize in curing cancer of the bank account. I help businesses quickly create extra income sources for their products via Internet sales."

Know what motivates people. Always focus on the benefits of your product or opportunity. Newbies tend to rely on communicating all the product features. People just don't care what's in your cookies or how you made them. They are more interested in knowing if they are low in cholesterol, chemical free and taste good.

"I help people improve their health and increase their energy levels with all natural liquid supplements."

"I specialize in helping people quickly create a secondary income stream with a very small investment of both time and money."

Your prospects are always asking themselves, "What's in it for me?" That's the question you should always focus on answering. Here's a warning that's an oldie but goody: "It's not how your product came to be but what it does for you and me."

Do You Know How? …What I Do Is

Every network marketer (and every business person) should be prepared with a well-crafted response to the, "What do you do?" question. It can do wonders for your posture and confidence as well as your prospecting results.

This revealing exercise can help you craft your own Twenty-Second Sizzle Message or response to, "What do you do for a living?"

Sit down with two blank pieces of paper or two blank computer pages. At the top of the first page write the heading: **Do You Know How**? At the top of the second page write the heading: **What I Do Is**.

Under the "**Do You Know How**?" heading describe 8-10 of the top problems or pains that your customers experience –

especially the ones that your product, service or opportunity solve. These are the "customer pains" you resolve.

Under the "**What I Do Is**" list how your product, service or opportunity solves the problems or pains. These are your "pain solutions" and how you serve people.

Once you have your list of "pains and solutions," you've created several possible answers for a well-crafted response to the "What do you?" question.

EXAMPLE:

Prospect: *"So, what do you do (for a living)?"*

Me: *"Do you know how there's millions of people that would love to own their business, perhaps work from home, be their own boss, own their time, but they're afraid to sell, they don't want to talk to family or strangers about business, they don't know what to say or how to say it…or even get started?"*

Prospect: *"Yes, I do."*

Me: *"Well, I'm an author, teacher and coach …and what I do is show people the amazing art of "conversational selling." I teach people a model of prospecting that's so simple and easy to learn, almost anyone can quickly begin to promote any product, service or opportunity they choose …and they can build an outrageously successful business."*

Another example:

Prospect: *"So, what do you do (for a living)?"*

You: *"Well, do you know how in this economy many people are without jobs, and many who have jobs are still underemployed and just can't save money for their children's college or for the future?"*

Prospect: "*Yes.*"

You: "*Well, what I do is (teach people how they can create a substantial second income stream, part-time, mostly using the internet.)*"

Or, "*Well, what I do is (show people how they can create a part time, home-based business that can make money for them while they sleep.)*"

When you offer a pain and a solution the person can relate to they'll usually let you know, and you may have a pre-qualified prospect. You've hit the mark when the person who asked comes back with something like, "*Hmm, tell me more,*" or,

"*That's interesting, tell me how you do that.*"

Here's a small step you can add to your response to determine if the person is simply making conversation or has a true interest in learning more.

EXAMPLE:

Prospect: "*Sue, what do you do (for a living)?*"

You: "*I own my own business.*"

Prospect: "*Oh, what kind of business?*" If they *don't* ask you about your business you know they may be not interested in a meaningful conversation.

You: "*Well, do you know how some people know they aren't getting everything they need from their diet and should be eating healthier, but just don't have the time to figure it all out?*"

Prospect: "*Yes I do.*"

You: *"Well, what I do is (show people how they can get most if not all the nutrients they need from a liquid nutritional supplement that's super healthy, affordable and great tasting.)"*

Again, if they are a prospect and you've piqued their interest, they'll likely ask you a few more questions. If not, don't press them.

Just keep polishing and refining your, **"Do you know how**? ...**What I do is**," response until you are completely comfortable with the flow – and more often than not people will be saying, "Hmm...tell me more."

The Five P's – Why People Buy

Understanding why people buy can help you craft and refine your sizzle message and responses. There are five basic motives that summarize the reasons people buy.

1. Profit: People want gain, achievement, profit or monetary benefit.

2. Pleasure: Pleasure can be comfort, convenience, affection, recognition, enjoyment, beauty, attraction, and luxury.

3. Peace of Mind: People want a service that guards their interests, their property, their health, their future security and their loved ones.

4. Pain: Most people want to avoid pain from hunger, poverty, illness, conflict with others and even the pain of change.

5. Pride: People have an inborn need for approval, acceptance, affection, admiration, and an advancement of their skills, lifestyle, reputation or simply the feeling that they are in charge of their lives.

Learn to design your approach, your intention and your questions so you are helping people achieve one or more of the 5 P's of *their* buying motivations.

Third Party Validation Is More Believable

Use third-party examples or stories rather than hyperbole. People don't tend to believe statements such as, "It's so great, …it's so amazing," "unbelievable" …they sound like hype.

Instead, show how others love your product or service. Look for opportunities to add credibility from third-party endorsements or testimonials, and make sure that they're real, specific and truthful.

Which response is more believable and credible?

(1) Customer: *"How's the lunch special today?"* Waiter: *"It's fantastic. Out of this world!"*

(2) Customer: *"How's the lunch special today?"* Waiter: "*Glad you asked. The couple that just left said it was one of the best meals they've ever had in our restaurant."*

Did you meet the couple? No. Do you know the couple? No, but the second response is more believable. Why? It came from a third party. Of course, make sure your response is also the truth.

Be aware of your audience. You may want to have a few different twenty-second sizzle intros based on who asks you, "What do you do?" Much of your intro depends on where you want to take a conversation with a prospect – product or business?

If you don't have a lot of information, you may want to keep your statement very general. However, if you're speaking with people who are looking for a home-based business or extra cash flow, you can offer a sizzle intro that leads with your opportunity rather than your product.

"I'm David Ward. I'm in the business of helping people work from their home and make extra income."

"My name is Dave Hernandez. I'm in the business of helping people find natural and more holistic solutions to their health challenges."

Always keep in mind your intention and the number one goal of network marketing – *helping and serving people*!

The Power of Active Listening

The best-kept, under-used and misunderstood secret of effective communication is listening. It's much more difficult to help and serve people if you don't know what they want, need or don't want. In order to learn what's important to people, you have to learn to communicate in ways that are effective.

Most people think about talking when they think of communicating. However, one study on listening showed that typical adults spend about 70% of their waking time hours communicating with others and broke it down into these proportions:

Writing – 9%
Reading – 16%
Talking – 30%
Listening – 40%

If we spend that much of our lives listening, then we should be great at it. Right?

Unfortunately so many of us *hear but don't listen* for full understanding. Hearing is passive. Listening is active and requires our full attention.

Here's an acronym that will help improve your "prospecting listening" and will support your intention to help people. The goal is to see if your product, service or opportunity is an appropriate match with their need.

LISTEN – **Learn** to **Invite Smartly** by **Tactfully Encouraging Need**

An interesting change of perspective is to think of your business as an "invitation business." As a good listener you are inviting people to share their concerns, wants and needs and then inviting them to review or consider your product service or opportunity as a possible solution.

If there is one single non-biological urge that all people have, and it's *to feel important*. How can you help people feel important? Ask questions and allow them to talk and express themselves. Once you know what is on their mind, what they need or want, then you can "smartly" (and strategically) "invite" them to review, sample, buy, experience or consider your product or opportunity.

Here are six ways to improve your listening and communication skills:

1. Talk less. Limit your own talking. It's impossible to listen and talk at the same time

2. Don't interrupt. Even a pause doesn't mean your prospect has exhausted a subject

3. Listen for their problems, wants and needs. Make this your most important objective while you're listening

4. Listen actively by occasionally providing feedback. Prove you're listening by saying, "Yes, I understand," "So what you're saying is…," "Tell me more about that…" "It seems like *(FILL IN THE BLANK)* is important to you."

5. Shut out external distractions and self-talk. Your prospect will know immediately if you are mentally somewhere else.

6. Listen for ideas, not just the words. Ask yourself, "What idea is the prospect trying to put across?"

If you feel that you understand the point the person is making, you may want to paraphrase and repeat their point. Then ask your prospect to confirm that you do indeed understand the point they're making.

The bible says, "Ask and you shall receive." The Network Marketing bible says, "Listen and learn to ask great questions, and then you shall receive."

Clarifying Questions – Helping People Move Forward

Here are two simple communication techniques you can use over and over again in a variety of conversations to determine a prospect's interest in moving forward.

These are not sales tricks or gimmicks. These are appropriate communication phrases that will help you discover where you are in the prospecting communications process. Have you met their needs? Do they require more information? Have you solved their concern? Have you handled their objections and, if so, are they ready to make decisions or take the next steps?

You are not trying to convince them of anything. You are "taking the lead" in the communications by helping them get clarity in their decision-making.

1. "If you knew for sure *(FILL IN THE BLANK)"*

In order to ask this, you have to "fill in the blank" based on what the prospect has told you about their needs. The "blank" is their condition being met.

For example: that this *"would meet your financial goals, ...help you sleep better and give you more energy, ...help you achieve your dreams, ...give you more free time with your family, ...get over your fear of selling, ...provide you with the Plan-B we talked about,"* etc.

You also must *dovetail your outcome;* meaning, state what you'd like them to do as a result of the condition being met.

"If you knew for sure *(FILL IN THE BLANK)* "

"...Would you be ready to get started tonight?"
"...Would you be ready to learn next steps?"
"...Would you be ready to try the product today?"
"...Would you be ready to join our team now?"
"...What would you say?"

Here's a non-network marketing industry example that should help you understand the simplicity and effectiveness of, "***If you knew for sure***.

"If you knew for sure we could get the financing at the rate you said you want, with no down payment, which is also what you asked for, would you be ready to drive this car home to your family tonight?"

"If you knew for sure" is a powerful yet appropriate communication tool that will help you determine a prospect's true interest based on what they've told you and the conditions (of what they told you) being met. It can also help lead them to making a decision on your suggested outcome.

"If you knew for sure (FILL IN THE BLANK) get started tonight?"

"If you knew for sure (FILL IN THE BLANK) join our team today?"

Monte Taylor, Jr.

A variation would be to end your question with, *"What would you say?"* to provide the prospect with a softer, perhaps more open-ended response.

"If you knew for sure (FILL IN THE BLANK) what would you say?"

"If I could show you (FILL IN THE BLANK) what would you say?"

2. "If I could show you *(FILL IN THE BLANK)"*

"If I could show you a plan where you could make back your original investment in your starter kit in 30 days, plus a profit…."

… Would you be ready to get started tonight?"
… Would you be ready to learn next steps?"
… Would you be ready to join our team?"
… What would you say?"

Here's a **simple truth**: In order to help people get clarity, reduce angst and perhaps save everyone's time, you need to provide leadership and positive closure to ALL your prospecting communications.

Don't forget, most people are "silently begging to be led."

What's Your Financial Freedom Number?

This is an effective visualization or "fast forward" exercise to help people imagine what it would be like to have an income stream that covered every expense they had, plus some extra. It works well in small or large group settings as well as in one-on-one communications. Here's what I say to introduce the exercise:

"Would everyone do me a small favor? Please think about your 'financial freedom number' for just a moment."

In a one-on-one or phone conversation I'll say this: *"I'm curious. Have you ever decided on your 'financial freedom number'?"*

Of course, most people don't know exactly what I mean at first, so I explain.

"Here's what I mean. Take a moment to think about how much money you'd need coming in to your checking/savings account automatically every month, year in and year out, to cover every expense you have. Everything! Then add another 30% on top for any extras, savings, vacations or whatever."

I'll give an example; *"If you need $10,000 to cover everything, multiply it by 30% to get another $3,000. Add those together and your number is $13,000."*

"Now that you've a moment to think about it, what's YOUR financial freedom number?"

You can use this exercise in large and small presentations, home business mixers and one-on-one presentations. **Never, ever** promise people or guarantee they can achieve their number. But offer this instead:

"Bill, if you have a genuine desire for change in your life and you're willing to put forth the effort, then imagine if in the next 24 to 36 months, working together, we could achieve your number."

"Imagine if you could join the tens of thousands of networking professional that are earning full-time incomes with part-time effort.

"Bill, what would you say?"

This exercise almost never fails to create a positive buzz and get people thinking and dreaming. It is especially effective when you can give a person the *specifics* of approximately how many customers and/or team members they would have to have in their business in order to achieve their "number." Be sure you have accurate information from your company.

Always ask people politely if they're willing to share their "number" with the group. If no one will share, use your own financial freedom number for the example.

Never make promises or guarantees you can't keep. *Never make income projections* or suggest that everyone in network marketing is getting filthy rich. It's simply not true.

What is true is that there are millions of network marketers enjoying extra incomes (part-time) and many thousands of network marketing professionals earning full-time incomes – some even *extraordinary* incomes.

CHAPTER TWELVE

Is It Really Cheaper To Pay The Bully?

"After a lifetime of choosing between comfort and risk, we are left with the life we currently have– and it was all of our choosing."
– Peter McWilliams

In his book, *Fuzzy Memories*, Jack Handey wrote, "There used to be this bully who would demand my lunch money every day. Since I was smaller, I would give it to him. Then I decided to fight back. I started taking karate lessons, but the instructor wanted $5 a lesson. I soon realized it was cheaper to pay the bully, so I gave up karate."

His point: "Too many of us believe it's easier to pay the bully than learn how to defeat the bully."

Perhaps the worst bullies are those that show up *after* our school lives have ended. Not the "people" kind, although there are those too, but the kind that show up as the things we avoid in everyday life – the things we fear or ignore.

Most people live a life on a singular path…too afraid to explore any other. Perhaps it's the fear of learning a new skill, trying something different, taking a chance and reaching out to a new person. Sometimes it's that "internal bullying voice"– the one that whispers in our ear, "What would others think?"

Maybe it's being too afraid to admit that you have a dream – a heart's desire – something you'd love to pursue if that "fear bully" wasn't always pushing us around. So we submit to honoring our "comfortableness" more than we honor our dreams.

Why would we do this when there's so much good news about dreams?

Simply by pursuing any one dream we can begin to find fulfillment. We don't need to pursue all of them. We don't even have to achieve the dream to find fulfillment – we can begin to find satisfaction just by actively pursuing it.

By living our dreams we can contribute not just to ourselves but also to everyone and everything around us.

With all of this good news, why aren't more of us living and pursuing our dreams?

Because we let our fear of being uncomfortable bully and push us around. Even contemplating a new action we feel fear, guilt, unworthiness – all of those things we generally think of as being "uncomfortable." Then we begin to look for things outside of ourselves to blame.

So many people with dreams of owning their own business, owning their life and their own time have said, "Just show me what to do …tell me what to say …I'll do whatever it takes."

Then after just one or two (often friends or relatives) reject their overtures or ask them – "Is this network marketing?" or, "Is this one of those pyramids?" or say, "Those things never work" – they'll run for the hills screaming, "It's just to difficult!"

And the bully wins!

I understand. In the beginning, when I first started my first network marketing business over twenty years ago, many people said "No" to me. (Some said, "Yes," but frankly, more said, "No").

And over time I began to recognize…

1. No matter what I did or said, or how good my product or opportunity was, some people said no. It's just the way it is.

2. I was going to have to learn some new skills and be willing to be "uncomfortable" (for a while) while I was practicing, improving, and refining my communications.

3. Once I began to learn the principles of service-based, *intentional conversations* – discovering a person's needs and desires to learn if I could serve them – more and more people began to say, "Yes." My confidence and my results began to improve greatly.

I also learned that one of the toughest things to sacrifice is the idea that we should *be comfortable* all the time. The irony is that the very feelings we have, and that occasional, often yucky *uncomfortableness* are among the very tools we need to realize our dreams.

If you're going to sacrifice anything, sacrifice your need to always feel comfortable.

My hope is that you find the principles, ideas, the model and scripts here useful – and in some fashion inspiring, too.

My wish is that you gain the confidence you need in yourself and in your prospecting skills to achieve extraordinary results in all your communications, relationships, and ultimately your business.

Moreover, as you pursue your goals and dreams, I implore you to never give up – and *absolutely* refuse to pay the bully.

Monte Taylor, Jr.

How To Get More Information From The Author

If you have a favorite prospecting script or story you'd like to share, please feel free to contact me through my website: www.montetaylor.com

I'd enjoy hearing from you.

FREE VIDEOS LINKED TO THIS BOOK!!!

To receive free "off the grid," prospecting and business building tips, more scripts," plus a FREE video series designed to help you get full value from this book, go to this web address below to subscribe and get immediate access. www.montetaylor.com/freestuff

My Very Best Wishes For Your Great Success!

Monte Taylor, Jr.

Made in the USA
Lexington, KY
25 August 2013